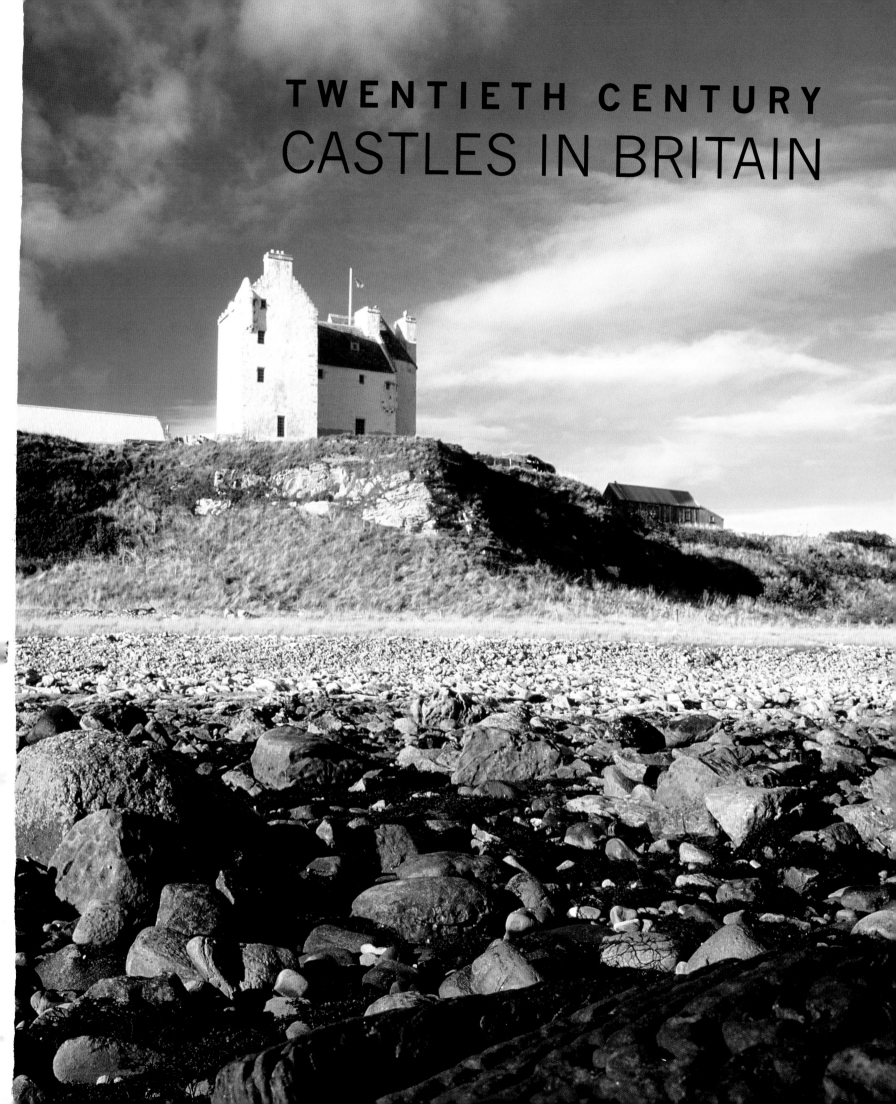

TWENTIETH CENTURY
CASTLES IN BRITAIN

TWENTIETH CENTURY
CASTLES IN BRITAIN

Amicia de Moubray

F

FRANCES LINCOLN LIMITED
PUBLISHERS

To Richard, with love

Now what doth Lady Alice so late on the turret stair,
Without a lamp to light her, but the diamond in her hair,
When every arching passage overflows with shallow gloom,
And dreams float through the castle into every silent room?

From William Allingham, 'Lady Alice'[1]

Frances Lincoln Limited
www.franceslincoln.com

Twentieth Century Castles in Britain
Copyright © Frances Lincoln Limited 2013
Text copyright © Amicia de Moubray 2013
Illustrations copyright © as listed on page 199
First Frances Lincoln edition 2013

A catalogue record for this book is available from the
British Library.

ISBN 978-0-7112-3178-8

Printed and bound in China

1 2 3 4 5 6 7 8 9

ENDPAPERS Drawing by Philip Tilden for the
proposed castle at Hengistbury Head, Hampshire,
commissioned by Gordon Selfridge.
PAGE 1 Ballone, near Tain, north of Inverness,
restored from a derelict ruin by Lachlan Stewart.
PAGE 2 Garden building designed by Sir Basil Spence
at Broughton Place, Peeblesshire.
RIGHT Castell Gyrn, Denbighshire, built in 1977.

CONTENTS

INTRODUCTION

A love of castles is deeply rooted in the British psyche. Children encounter castles from an early age, enjoying them in fairy stories, which abound with images of castles, as in the Sleeping Beauty, in other fiction – Hogwarts Castle of Harry Potter fame must be one of the famous castles in the world – and in history books. They enjoy being transported to an imaginary medieval world evoked by the idea of a castle: small girls adore dressing up as princesses and boys like donning knights' attire. They build sandcastles, many of them complete with moats, and play on climbing frames resembling castles. Castles feature in several playground games such as 'I'm the King of the Castle, Get down you dirty rascal'.

Castles are also part of our psyche because they are an integral part of our architectural history: from the early fortifications erected by the Normans to the fanciful wedding-cake gothic creations of the eighteenth century, castles in every sort of state of repair are to be found scattered over England, Scotland and Wales. The castle is part of the popular image of Scotland, from the early brochs (round hollow towers) to nineteenth-century baronial castles bristling with turrets. The north coast of North Wales and the Cheshire borders in particular have a thrillingly rich medley of castles spanning several hundred years, from medieval structures to whimsical nineteenth-century castellated confections.

In essence a castle (from the Latin word *castellum*) is a fortified dwelling intended for purposes of residence and defence. It is thus a potent symbol of power and achievement. Possession of a castle has been throughout the centuries a symbol of success, because of the association of a castle, large, strong, secure and prominent, with power and status. In Norman England the castle was the epicentre of administration of a large area presided over by an almost omnipotent nobleman surrounded by his serfs. Until the industrial revolution castles, along with the great cathedrals and monasteries, dominated the land. To this day castles, with a few exceptions such as Braylsham Castle (see page 172), are positioned on raised sites, which accentuate their importance. In imitation of this association with power, there are houses that bear no resemblance at all to castles but are called Castle Something.

The British enthusiasm for castles is perhaps especially characteristic of an island race. A castle surrounded by a moat is after all a miniature version of a country surrounded by sea. Castles reflect the deep-rooted need for security of islanders; and, as implied by the dictum 'an Englishman's home is his castle', a castle is a place of refuge and safety, where a man can do as he wishes.

LEFT Braylsham Castle, Sussex, designed by John Mew in the 1990s.

Over time the term castle has evolved to mean any structure that sports all or some of the architectural features associated with castles, such as machicolations, turrets or bartizans. John Goodall, in his magisterial tome *The English Castle*, which charts its history from 1066 to the Civil War of the 1640s, defines the castle as 'the residence of a lord made imposing through the architectural trappings of fortification'.[2]

As well as being symbols of power, through their association with the past – real or implied by their features – castles have an intensely romantic and enduring appeal. But while some retain their grandeur, haughtily surveying their surroundings, others are mere shards of their past splendour, wrapped around and interspersed with buildings which have arrived later on the scene in villages and towns, peering somewhat forlornly out from these surroundings, as does, for example, Sutton Valence in Kent. Such ruins nonetheless have an appeal of their own, in conjuring up the spirit of the past.

For those of a heightened romantic persuasion the chance to rescue a ruined castle and bring it back to life after centuries of woeful neglect is the ultimate fantasy. Adam Nicolson encapsulates the sentiments of many a would-be castle-restorer when summing up his grandmother Vita Sackville-West's restoration of Sissinghurst Castle: 'there was a chance here to revitalize a once-great but deeply neglected place, to take a ruin and make it flower.'[3] For such people the prospect of living in a castle drenched in history is immensely attractive. It offers both a beguiling form of escapism and a tangible link with the past.

The desire to build and restore castles has continued into the twentieth century and beyond. This book looks at some of the sparkling new castles that were built after 1900, and at restorations of crumbling ancient structures that in effect turned them into something new – and therefore might also be called 'a twentieth-century castle'.

Understandably castles in most people's minds are inextricably entwined with the feudal Middle Ages, but in fact they were first introduced to Britain by the Normans. Examples of the Normans' motte and bailey castles can be seen in the Bayeux tapestry. Quick and inexpensive to build, they offered good protection, comprising a timber tower on top of an earthen mound surrounded by an inner palisade and a ditch (from which the earth had been dug for the mound), which as the design of castles evolved was utilized as a moat. The whole defensive area comprised the bailey, which consisted of a larger but lower enclosure, also surrounded by an inner palisade and ditch in which were the domestic buildings, including the lord's private quarters, a great hall and shelter for his men in time of danger. The bailey and the motte were linked by a timber bridge. Cocooned within their defensive castles, the Norman barons were able to exert their power over the Anglo-Saxons.

Gradually stone began to replace timber as the preferred building material. Throughout the twelfth century imposing stone keeps with exceptionally thick walls became an integral component of a castle. It was at this time that many of the architectural accoutrements traditionally associated with castle architecture were first employed, including portcullises, machicolations in the entrance passages and arrow-loops. As the castles became increasingly sophisticated so in parallel did the mechanics of siege engineers. Each side was trying to outwit the other. Stone therefore replaced timber as the building material for the palisades of the bailey, often with stone towers built at intervals to ensure a better look-out system as well as to provide increased protection from poundings from weapons such as catapults and the lethal pivotal-beam trebouchets. Although the thirteenth century is regarded as the golden age of castle building as, in the words of John Goodall, 'the architect laboured in stone for the king and England's greatest magnates to defeat the ingenuity of the siege engineer',[4] the expense of stone limited the numbers of castles constructed.

Much has been written in the last few decades about whether medieval English castles were primarily built as defensive castles or houses. As Robert Liddiard states, 'rather than judging castles as military buildings, the historiographical trend is now to see them as noble residences built in the military style'.[5]

A similar debate surrounds the Scottish castle and tower house. Charles McKean explores it in *The Scottish Chateau: The Country House of Renaissance Scotland*, published in 2001. 'The predominant Victorian perception of pre-1707 Scotland was of a country isolated from the mainstream European Renaissance, turned in on itself and continuing anachronistically to build castles when mansions, country houses and villas were being constructed elsewhere. That perception remained current until towards the end of the twentieth century.' The jury is still out on this question. For instance, T.M. Devine, writing in 1999, states: 'the tower house, designed mainly for defence'.[6] McKean argues that chateau is the correct appellation, even though he acknowledges that 'Scottish aristocrats have a tendency to rename their seats castles at the slightest opportunity.'

Two types of Scottish tower houses predominate. The L-plan castle was first introduced in the fifteenth century when it became fashionable for a wing to be added to an existing

LEFT Coxton Tower, a fine example of a seventeenth-century Scottish tower house near Elgin, Moray.

LEFT Mock 'medieval' kennels for
the Fitzwilliam hounds at Milton,
Peterborough, probably designed
by Sir William Chambers.

tower, usually at right angles to provide extra living space. Z-plan castles are invariably a composite structure featuring a round tower on one corner and a square or rectangular one on the other.

In the next phase, sometimes referred to as 'the twilight age of castles', in the late fourteenth and early fifteenth centuries castles became primarily country houses masquerading as splendid castles – for instance Bodiam Castle in Sussex, 'a residence made architecturally magnificent through the trappings of fortification'.[7]

Around the time of the Civil War, castles appeared to become no longer fashionable emblems of aristocracy but what John Goodall describes as 'architectural enemies of peace and the Commonwealth'[8] – relics of an old and anachronistic order. The Civil War was responsible for a break with the past in all spheres of cultural, social and political life. 'In the course of a decade [castles] that had been adapted over centuries as great residences were deliberately demolished and their remains left to ruin.'[9] With the restoration of the monarchy a preference for a new classical order prevailed. Castle building went out of vogue for some fifty years until the architect Sir John Vanbrugh built himself a small castle in Greenwich in 1718–19. Its avant-garde asymmetrical outline was a precursor of the picturesque castles that would be found in late eighteenth-century landscaped parks. Many of these were deliberately built in a semi-ruinous state, their purpose being to conjure up a romantic idyll and for the antiquarian imagination

RIGHT Eastnor Castle,
Herefordshire, designed by
Sir Robert Smirke and finished
in 1825.

a link with the past – for example, the castle by Sanderson Miller in the park at Hagley in Worcestershire. The fortunate Fitzwilliam family's hounds had kennels built for them – probably to a design by Sir William Chambers – that were bedecked with towers and a castellated and bastioned screen at Milton near Peterborough.

For the eighteenth-century Scottish landowner, castles were redolent of what Stephen Astley describes as 'a golden past of a country ruled by Scottish Kings and associated with all the chivalric trappings of a romantic medievalism'.[10] In the mid-eighteenth century the 3rd Duke of Argyll demolished his old castle at Inveraray, replacing it with a new one designed by Roger Morris and built by William Adam, father of Robert Adam. As a castle, not a classical mansion, it proudly proclaimed the Duke's ancient lineage. As William's health declined, his sons, Robert and John, took over his work on numerous castles, including Stirling, Edinburgh and Duart Castles as well as the great Scottish military forts such as Fort George constructed by the British in the wake of the 1745 rebellion. Thereafter the Scots enjoyed a new prosperity and confidence and many

ABOVE A watercolour by James Henry Nixon (1802–57) of a scene from the Eglington Tournament held in Ayrshire in 1839.

Scottish aristocrats turned to the Adam brothers either to remodel their existing castles – such as Culzean Castle, Ayrshire, rebuilt for the 10th Earl of Cassillis – or to build new ones. It is a rarely explored aspect of the Adams' work that more than 10 per cent of their projects were in the 'castle style'. Castles were 'emblems of historical continuity, either nationally as symbols of a Scottish kingdom or locally in terms of the continuity of land ownership'.[11]

Separately, the eighteenth century also saw the emergence of gothic, a light-hearted version of the medieval style of architecture. Horace Walpole, author of the first gothic novel, *The Castle of Otranto*, published in 1746, transformed a modest seventeenth-century house – Strawberry Hill in Twickenham, Middlesex. While not strictly a castle, this was an eminent example of a whimsical style that included pinnacles, battlements and windows with gothic fenestration. He often referred to it as his 'gothic castle'. Another example of Strawberry Hill Gothic was the long demolished Pomfret Castle in Piccadilly, London, built in 1756–9, just behind where the Ritz Hotel now stands.

The end of the Napoleonic Wars brought on a sudden burst of euphoric castle building throughout the British Isles. A new castle was for an aristocrat a symbolic way of demonstrating rank and a newfound confidence in an era of peace. Eastnor Castle near Ledbury, designed by Sir Robert Smirke for the Earl Somers and finished in 1825, is a particularly brilliant example of this trend. Solid and massive, and visible from afar, it was a statement of the social supremacy of the Somers family.

A mania for the Middle Ages characterized the age. Sir Walter Scott played a crucial role in this: his writings had an enormous impact on the drama, literature and painting of the day – in particular his *Waverley* novels, the first of which was published in 1814. The Eglington Tournament, an extraordinary medieval-style tournament in Ayrshire in 1839, attended by scores of aristocrats dressed in armour and medieval-style outfits, helped to promulgate the fashion. The fervour for medieval armour was widespread: country-house displays of armour were the nineteenth-century equivalent of the sculpture galleries of the eighteenth-century milordi.

The opening up of Scotland with the advent of the railway, the vogue for Sir Walter Scott's novels and Queen Victoria's purchase of Balmoral all helped fuel demand for Scottish castles. By the end of the nineteenth century the Highlands were awash from glen to glen with all manner of elaborate medieval-style baronial confections sprouting turrets and battlements.

South of the border it was the scions of old families who enthusiastically embraced medievalism, flaunting their ancient lineage by aggrandizing their existing country houses and restoring castles in the medieval style. One such scion was the 3rd Marquess of Bute, reputedly the world's wealthiest man, who was described on his death in 1900 by *The Tablet* as a man who 'loved the past and lived in it'. He employed the idiosyncratic architect William Burges to carry out an exotic restoration of Cardiff Castle and at the same time (1871–2) to draw up plans for restoring both Rothesay Castle on the Isle of Bute and Castell Coch, just outside Cardiff. At the time Bute was only twenty-four, and he had first met Burges, who was twenty years older, six years earlier. According to his biographer, J. Mordaunt Crook, they were both 'born romantics, drunk with learning, in love with the Middle Ages'. Rothesay remained unaltered but Burges transformed Castell Coch 'from a heap of rubble [into] a fairy-tale castle which seems almost to have materialized from the pages of a medieval manuscript'.[12]

Arundel Castle in Sussex is the supreme example of a Victorian transformation of a castle on a vast scale. In 1868 the 15th Duke of Norfolk came of age, eight years after the death of his father, who had begun an extensive programme of alterations to the castle, including the addition of a large octagonal armoury. At the time of his death only a Norman-style gateway had been completed. The 15th Duke, keen to continue the reconstruction, employed a fellow Catholic, J.C. Buckler (1824–1904), who skilfully transformed the castle into a monumental edifice with a splendid 133 foot/40-metre-long barons' hall that dominates the surrounding countryside and town, to borrow the words of H.V. Morton, 'like a trumpeter on a hill'.[13]

Between 1844 and 1850 the 1st Lord Tollemache employed the architect Anthony Salvin, who had already worked for him at Helmingham Hall, the ancient Suffolk seat of the Tollemaches, to design Peckforton Castle in Cheshire. Superbly situated, looking across to the ruins of the thirteenth-century Beeston Castle, Peckforton is a dramatic sight. Built in the medieval style, and costing £68,000, it is the most accurate of all the Victorian 'medieval castles'. By the 1840s, the vogue for 'sham castles' such as Eastnor having waned, it was generally only acceptable for aficionados to construct a castle strictly adhering to architectural scholarship, as was the case at Peckforton, to avoid any censure. Lord Tollemache, in his youth a champion athlete, had twenty-four children, drove a four-in-hand in his eighties and ruled over his tenants on his 26,000-acre/10,521-hectare estates like a Norman baron presiding in his great castle.

This, in a nutshell, was the background to the enthusiasm for castles in the twentieth century – as castles saved, castles restored and castles built.

CASTLES SAVED

A man who was extremely influential in in the twentieth-century story of the castle was Lord Curzon, another great worshipper of the past: 'To me the past is sacred',[14] he wrote. Kenneth Rose, one of his many biographers, claims that 'Kedleston [his family's seat in Derbyshire] never ceased to haunt Curzon's heart and mind during his seven years [as Viceroy] in India,'[15] but he was not to inherit until the advanced age of fifty-seven. This perhaps explains his pursuit of rescuing castles. His passion for the preservation of monuments and buildings stemmed from the time he spent in India, from 1898 to 1905. Appalled by the casual attitude of both the British and the Indians to the care of India's ancient monuments, he helped to awaken the Indians' consciousness of their outstanding architectural treasure heritage. On his return to England he was to play a key part in alerting widespread public opinion to the growing need to save and preserve ancient buildings. 'Beautiful and ancient buildings which recall the life and customs of the past are not only historical documents of supreme value but are part of the spiritual and aesthetic heritage of a nation, imbuing it with reverence and educating

LEFT Tattershall Castle,
Lincolnshire, valiantly rescued
by Lord Curzon.

LEFT The conservation
architect William Weir, whom
Lord Curzon employed to
work on both Tattershall and
Bodiam Castles.

its taste,'[16] he wrote in his will. Anyone who loves England and its rich architectural tapestry should salute him for saving two of its important castles, Bodiam and Tattershall.

The saving of the fifteenth-century Tattershall Castle in Lincolnshire was an early conservation *cause célèbre*. In the autumn of 1911 a row arose over the sale of the castle and four of its important fifteenth-century fireplaces, which had inspired Pugin's designs for the fireplaces in the Palace of Westminster. The day after an unknown American millionaire had signed the purchase contract the council of the relatively new National Trust met to discuss whether or not to buy it. Despite the generous offer of an interest-free loan by Sir Francis Trippel, the members voted against the acquisition, largely because, astonishingly, an appeal launched by the National Trust to raise funds to save the castle had met with little enthusiasm. It was rumoured that the castle was to be knocked down and shipped brick by brick to America, and that 'the fireplaces are in actual process of being prised out . . . for removal . . . – where? We know not whether to some millionaire's hotch-potch of curios in America or to some dealer's warehouse in England,' wrote an incensed Colonel Henry Knollys to *The Times* on 11 September 1911.

A few weeks later it emerged that Lord Curzon had courageously bought the 2,000-acre/809-hectare estate. *Country Life* played a pivotal role in the tale, for it was seeing pictures of the castle in the magazine that prompted Curzon to visit it the very same day. When he saw it, he recorded, he bared his head as he looked down on the river and fields and said, 'the vandals shall not have it'.[17] By 5 pm he had sent a telegram to say he would buy it and save it for the nation.

Curzon's intention was reported as being to restore the castle, transforming it into the 'showplace of Lincolnshire' to be visited by thousands of people. His keen appreciation of beauty and sense of place led him to stipulate the purchase of a certain field as a condition of the sale to prevent it being built on. This also enabled him to restore the moat by letting water in from the canal in the field, which cost him an extra £295.

Fortuitously he was able to buy back the fireplaces; he had discovered them, packed up ready for export, in an antique dealer's in Bayswater in 1912. Their return to Tattershall was a magnificently orchestrated event: a splendid procession of five lorries carrying the fireplaces, each drawn by two gaily decorated horses passing under triumphal arches of flowers and bunting, processed through decorated streets for an hour and a half. A Union Jack proudly flew over the rescued castle. Schoolchildren followed in wagons, and Curzon and the local vicar, the Reverend M. Yglesias, sat like potentates in an open landau drawn with ropes by several of the workmen who were already restoring the castle under the supervision of the architect William Weir (1865–1950), a pupil of Philip Webb.

The grand opening of the castle in 1915, after three years of restoration, at the height of the First World War, was an uplifting patriotic event. Curzon proclaimed the significance of buildings such as Tattershall in such turbulent times: 'They speak to us of the valour and strength of our ancestors.'[18] One can forgive this crusader for the preservation of old England – *Country Life* described him in 1914 as 'the one man in England who rose to the challenge of Tattershall' – for immortalizing himself at Tattershall in a set of stained glass depicting all the owners of the castle stretching back to the Earl of Tattershall in 1066.

That Bodiam Castle still rises serenely out of its broad moat deep in the Sussex countryside is also due to Lord Curzon's prescient imagination and generosity. He was bewitched by the ancient moated castle from the moment he first saw it, which was almost certainly in 1905. Setting his heart on acquiring it, that 'so rare a treasure should neither be lost to our country nor desecrated by irreverent hands',[19] he made an offer to the owner, Lord Ashcombe, but was turned down. Following Ashcombe's death some ten years later, Curzon bought it from Ashcombe's son in 1916. Characteristically

LEFT Bodiam Castle, Sussex, saved by Lord Curzon. He was bewitched by the ancient moated castle from the moment he first saw it.

sensitive to the *genius loci*, Curzon also bought a tranche of land surrounding the castle to protect its approach. This area he was to clear of its fences and hedges and plant with trees, creating a sylvan park-like setting that greatly enhances Bodiam's fairy-tale tranquillity.

Its magnificent setting is a major part of Bodiam's attraction: the sheer monumentality of the castle is accentuated by its reflection in the glassy, smooth waters of the generous moat surrounding it, the one enhancing the other. 'The first sight of Bodiam Castle has seemed to some people an experience almost as thrilling as the first sight of the Colosseum or the Taj Mahal,'[20] wrote a reviewer of Curzon's history of Bodiam, published shortly after his death in 1925, while his second wife described her first visit to Bodiam: 'Looking down on the castle was like looking into another world, I can find no words to describe the beauty . . . I felt, as I looked at this divinely inspired picture, that I dared not take my eyes off it, for fear that when I looked again it would have disappeared in a mist or a cloud – it could only be a fairy castle.'[21]

'To restore Bodiam to its original magnificence, so that its beauty might last forever,'[22] as his wife recalls, Curzon again turned to William Weir, who oversaw an extensive programme of archaeological excavations and repairs, which included

draining the moat, repairing the foundations and restoring the battlements, employing anything between fifteen and thirty or so men at a time over a period of fifteen months.

The Curzons briefly entertained the notion of moving into Bodiam. Architects' plans were drawn up but alas they are no longer extant. It is not clear why the Curzons eventually decided not to restore Bodiam as a dwelling but Lord Curzon candidly admits in his history of Bodiam, 'I desisted from what might have easily degenerated into an archaeological crime.'[23] Perhaps by that time, with his father having died in 1916, all his attention was focused on Kedleston and to pour money into the scheme seemed an extravagant folly.

Perhaps rather churlishly, Curzon's passion for country houses and castles was not always well received. Sir Mark Sykes drew a cartoon of a ragged Lord Curzon against a background of the noble buildings he had restored. On the pavement is his upturned cap and by his side a notice that reads 'kind frens pity mee i wos wons a viseroy but lost mi all bildin cassels and addin to the bewtis of ingland', while Count Carlo Sforza thought that Curzon's love of castles was evidence of a megalomaniacal streak within in his character. Nevertheless, every year thousands of visitors to Tattershall and Bodiam have reason to feel grateful to him, for he left

both castles to the nation in the care of the National Trust in his will. John Bailey, then chairman of the National Trust, called his donation 'the greatest individual gift'.

Another person who 'saved' a castle was Queen Elizabeth the Queen Mother. Four months after the death of her husband, George VI, in 1952, she went to stay with her close friends Commander and Lady Doris Vyner, in Caithness, the northernmost part of Scotland overlooking the Orkneys. One day while out for a drive they drove past the Castle of Mey (then known as Barrogill Castle), built between 1566 and 1572 by Sir George Sinclair, 4th Earl of Caithness, for his second son, William. Owned by Captain Imbert Terry, the castle had been up for sale for months; no buyers being forthcoming, its likely fate was imminent demolition. 'I thought this would be a terrible pity. One had seen so much destruction in one's life,' said the Queen Mother.[24] Occupied by Coastal Defence

troops during the Second World War and severely damaged by a wild storm in the winter of 1952, the castle was in a poor state without any modern conveniences. There was no running water or electricity; the Imbert Terrys had hip baths.

The Queen Mother was captivated by Caithness, saying that she slept more soundly there than anywhere else. Perhaps, too, castles held an appeal for her, as she had spent two or three months every summer at her family's Glamis Castle, Perthshire, in her childhood and she also inhabited Windsor and Balmoral Castles. Two months later she bought the castle for a nominal £100, having declined Captain Imbert Terry's generous offer of giving it to her. Commander Vyner

negotiated the purchase of some land stretching along the coast for £300: 'It would all work quite economically for you & although not a good shoot would amuse Your Majesty's guests & give food for the table.'[25]

The Queen Mother confided in her Treasurer, 'Do you think me mad?'[26] At that time, shortly after the war, it was cheaper to knock down an ancient castle than go to the expense of restoring one. Nevertheless, the fashionable London decorators Lenygon and Morant drew up a scheme for the decoration of the principal rooms and were responsible for many elements. In the 1950s many old large Caithness houses were being dismantled and the Queen Mother bought

OPPOSITE The staircase
in the entrance hall of the
Castle of Mey.

LEFT The Queen Mother
and a faithful corgi in
October 1955 on the
occasion of her first stay,
following the initial phase
of the renovation.

much of the furniture from Miss Miller Calder's saleroom in nearby Thurso, and also from the local antique shop, the Ship's Wheel. Where possible, she bought items linked with the castle such as two Sinclair Bibles and a great double-handed claymore. The first phase of the renovations were finished by 1955, when the Queen Mother first came to stay in the last week of her summer holidays in October. Work was completed in 1960.

In buying the castle the Queen Mother planned 'to escape there occasionally when life became hideous'. One of the great attractions of her annual summer holidays there was its isolation, 'at the furthest tip of these islands, one feels so beautifully far away and the newspapers come too late to be readable.' She loved to walk her corgis along the coast and visit her cattle, in which she took a great interest. Such was her love for the place that when her factor, Martin Leslie, visited in May, he had to ring her daily to report on 'how the people are, how the stock are looking and what Caithness is looking like.'[27] Thanks to the Queen Mother's restoration, today the Castle of Mey continues to enchant the thousands of visitors who flock to it during the summer months, when it is open to the public. The example of the Castle of Mey spawned several romantically led (Scottish) restorations 'in the Queen Mother's footsteps by private individuals'.[28]

LEFT Portrait by Robert
Sauber of Lord Howard de
Walden dressed in medieval
costume, which hangs in the
great hall of the Keep at Dean
Castle, Ayrshire.

CASTLES RESTORED

Some restorations were so comprehensive that effectively the result was a new building, though still with the stamp of a former age and emphatically with the stamp of a castle.

The magazine *Country Life*, established in 1897, played an important role in the story of the castle in Britain in the twentieth century. This was mainly because of the patronage and personal enthusiasm of the magazine's founder, Edward Hudson, who himself employed Lutyens to restore Lindisfarne Castle in Northumberland for his summer residence, and toyed with the idea of buying Lympne Castle in Kent. Hudson promoted a newly romantic vision of an older England that coincided with a burgeoning anti-industrial spirit prevalent amongst those *Country Life* was aimed it. Castles fitted that vision. In the magazine's pages were to be found advertisements for decaying castles offered for sale.

And there were plenty. 'The sound of the auctioneer's hammer is heard throughout the land, and everywhere estates are being broken up, divided into lots and sold to new owners,' wrote P.H. Ditchfield.[30] Nowhere was this trend more in evidence than in the south-east of England, where in the early years of the twentieth century five decrepit ancient castles – Leeds, Hever, Saltwood, Allington (all in Kent) and Herstmonceux (in Sussex) – were sold to new owners who took great delight in restoring them with swaggering Edwardian panache, giving them a new lease of life.

Interestingly the restoration of four of the five castles was financed by American money (Herstmonceux being the exception) to the horror of commentators who were mourning the death of the old social order: 'The power of the purse of American millionaires also tends greatly to the vanishing of much that is English – the treasures of English art, rare pictures and books, and even of houses,' lamented Ditchfield.[31]

The arriviste American pillaging his way into ancient strongholds of England was much derided at the time. A passage in Vita Sackville-West's novel *The Heir* is wonderfully evocative of such an arriviste: the butler describes what is in

The 8th Lord Howard de Walden (1880–1946) is the epitome of all twentieth-century castle enthusiasts. Passionate about the fourteenth century, he rented Chirk Castle in North Wales and restored Dean Castle in Kilmarnock, Ayrshire, which he inherited. It had been gutted by fire in 1735. Augustus John, when staying at Chirk, came down to breakfast one day to be greeted by the spectacle of Lord Howard de Walden sitting reading *The Times* in a suit of armour. He had had it specially made for him by Felix Joubert. 'It took six weeks to fit to him while he stood for several hours a day having it hammered to his exact measurements.'[29] A supremely wealthy man, Lord Howard de Walden spent almost forty years restoring the keep and the palace range at Dean Castle, even going so far as to reconstruct the fighting platforms around the courtyard walls and a new sixteenth-century-style gatehouse (1935–6). The castle is now a museum and still contains his extensive collection of armour and weaponry and his wife Margherita (Van Raalte)'s outstanding collection of musical instruments.

RIGHT Cartoon of Sir Martin
Conway from *The Times*,
November 1931.

THE CLIMBER.
" Fearless minds climb some day unto
crowns."—SHAKESPEARE (*modified*).
SIR MARTIN CONWAY.

fact a Brazilian visit but could easily be an American. 'Motoring parties . . . coming to look over the house, and making free of the place . . . They came in a big car . . . They said they should have thought that if anyone had a house to sell, he would have been only too glad to show parties over it, order or no order, they said, especially if the house was so unsalable, two hours by train from London and not up to date in any way . . . Very insolent sort of people they were, sir, I must say.'[32]

All five castles were in woefully poor condition, some, notably Allington and Herstmonceux, close to being beyond redemption. But all had a powerful intrinsic sense of ancient history, which no new castle built from scratch, however elaborate or historically correct, could ever possess. No wonder these castles appealed, particularly given their proximity to London.

Sir Martin Conway, later Lord Conway of Allington, a neighbour and friend of Edward Hudson's in Queen Anne's Gate in London, was a pivotal figure in the renaissance of the clutch of castles in the south-east. He was married to an American newspaper heiress, Katrina, the daughter of Charles Lambach of Maine, builder of the Chicago and Western railway, and the stepdaughter of Manton Marble, proprietor and editor of the *New York World*. Conway was responsible for the restoration of Allington Castle, largely bankrolled by Katrina and Manton Marble. Later in his long life, he married another American, Iva Lawson, the widow of Reginald Lawson; the Lawsons were briefly the owners of Herstmonceux Castle, before purchasing Saltwood Castle. He wrote for *Country Life* a series of articles on Leeds Castle in 1913 and Allington and Herstmonceux in 1918. During the war it became increasingly difficult for the magazine's architectural writers to travel around Britain, which curtailed the choice of houses to feature. Conway's first-hand acquaintance with his subjects must have been welcome. Moreover, what could be more patriotic than celebrating English castles at a time of war?

What fun castle enthusiasts must have had discussing their plans! Conway's diaries record several meetings with Claude Lowther who, before acquiring Herstmonceux Castle in 1911, lived at the Friars, a thirteenth-century cloisters that had been turned into a dwelling after the Reformation in Aylesford, just a couple of miles from Allington. 'Lowther came to lunch and we discussed restoration all afternoon,'[33] records Conway in his diary in March 1911.

A sense of history also appealed to an ever-burgeoning stream of new millionaires who began to infiltrate society in the twentieth century, such as Julius Drewe, who built Castle Drogo (see page 82) and Lord Armstrong, who restored Bamburgh Castle in the closing years of his long life (see page 30). Eager to adopt the life of the English country gentleman and to gain widespread social acceptance at any cost, and many of them keen to distance themselves from their industrial and mercantile origins, they were drawn to a deeply nostalgic vision of an older England far removed from that suggested by the self-aggrandizing newly built edifices of many Victorian industrialists. Castles fitted the bill perfectly. One of these self-aggrandizers was the enormously wealthy Sir Weetman Dickinson Pearson, later 1st Viscount Cowdray (1856–1927), who had become rich by constructing canals and railways all over the world as well as from oil exploration in Mexico. He bought the Cowdray Park estate in Sussex in 1908 and envisaged replacing the sprawling Victorian mansion with a 'new Cowdray Castle'.[34] But the First World War intervened and his ambition came to naught.

In Scotland, castles have always been laden with romantic associations and represent historical continuity. That is why both Duart Castle on the Isle of Mull and Eilean Donan in Kintail were rebuilt at the beginning of the twentieth century, and played a highly charged symbolic role in legendary clan gatherings just before the First World War.

Around the turn of the twentieth century there was a subconscious desire to find a national style that had historical precedents quite unlike the vulgarian overblown crenellations of many Scotch Victorian baronial piles. Scotland was rediscovering its Celtic past and there was growing interest in the clan and Gaelic cultures that had been stifled following the Forty-Five Rebellion. The sophisticated understated oeuvre of the Scottish architect Sir Robert Lorimer (1864–1929) is testimony to this prevailing feeling and his superb sensitive restoration of Dunderave on the shore of Loch Fyne is the quintessential example of the romanticist approach to architecture (see page 106). A worthy successor in the twenty-first century is the architect Lachlan Stewart, who imbues all his projects, whether restorations or new builds, with an equally discerning sensitivity and an underlying sense of Scottishness (see page 178).

The second half of the twentieth century saw a renaissance in the restoration of Scottish tower houses and castles, as evidenced by the newsletter of the Scottish Castles Association, which is always brimming with examples of tower houses or castles that have been restored in recent years. Following the Historic Buildings and Ancient Monuments Act of 1953 state grants became available for the first time through the auspices of the recently formed Historic Buildings for Scotland. From the late 1950s to the early 1990s more than seventy tower house grant-aided restorations came about. They are notable for their compactness in a largely servantless age.

Dunderave and Eilean Donan (see pages 106 and 120), apart from being intensely romantic castles that encapsulate the romance of the Highlands, make fascinating case studies in what constituted a sensitive restoration of the day. It is arguable whether today Lorimer would have been allowed to restore Dunderave or John MacRae Eilean Donan. But even as early as 1923 the restoration of Eilean Donan was proving to be controversial. The travel writer M.E.M. Donaldson wrote:

> On the first occasion we had been delighted and held by a picture perfect in every detail, for confronting us was the magnificent ruin of Eilean Donan, then the most picturesque I have seen on the castle-strewn shores of the west coast . . . but no such view is any longer obtainable. For returning several years later, I was horrified and repelled by the ruined picture which obtruded itself on the outraged surroundings, the remains of the castle being in the throes of a rebuilding which must permanently disfigure the landscape. In any modern rebuilding operations the end no less than the means to the end are alike hideous. From start to finish in the proceedings, everything is ugly and one can only marvel at a taste which finds any satisfaction in transforming a picturesque ruin which harmonizes so completely with its surroundings into a permanent blot on the landscape . . . How any one identified with the country by reason of his clan can thus choose to identify himself with a proceeding usually associated with Americans or vulgarians, passes comprehension.[35]

BELOW The stirring profile
of Eilean Donan Castle, which
was largely rebuilt in the early
twentieth century.

But as Lachlan Stewart says, 'Each generation has their own version of restoration, 'and inevitably each generation of restorers will attract critics from those who favour a purist approach.'[36] In November 1991 the Architectural Heritage Society of Scotland organized a conference entitled 'Restoring Scotland's Castles'. The papers illuminate the widespread debate that has raged in recent years on how far the restoration of what are now regarded as iconic Scottish ruins should go. Until the closing years of the twentieth century restorers had a more or less free hand and more than forty tower houses had been restored. Now Historic Scotland is in most instances antipathetic to restoration, unless every aspect of the restoration meets its exacting standards of academic purity.

But in an astonishing volte-face in 2011 Historic Scotland relented on its original ruling that Tioram Castle in the west Highlands should remain as 'a spectacular, complex and, apparently, untouched ruin'. The owner, Lex Brown, had doggedly persisted with all the relevant authorities for more than a decade in his request to be allowed to restore it as a habitable dwelling. Historic Scotland eventually agreed that, as Lex Brown records, 'in the light of Tioram's ongoing deterioration, a scheme for reoccupation is the only viable means to achieve its long-term preservation'.

LEFT Broughton Place, near Peebles in the
Scottish Borders, a modern interpretation of
a traditional Scottish tower house designed
by Sir Basil Spence in 1938.

BELOW Highfort Court (left) and Rochester
Court (right), eccentric blocks of flats in
Kingsbury, west London, designed by
Ernest Trobridge in the 1930s.

CASTLES BUILT

The story of the castle in the twentieth century is not just one of restoration: throughout the century, and into the next, new castles have continued to be built in Scotland, Wales and England.

The beginning of the century is dominated by the restorations of existing castles such as Lindisfarne in Northumberland (see page 62) and Allington in Kent (see page 74). The best known of the castles built from scratch is undoubtedly Sir Edwin Lutyens's great Castle Drogo in Devon (see page 82). And the least known is the odd Rivington Castle just outside Bolton (see page 114), deliberately built by Lord Leverhulme as a ruin.

Possibly the most eccentric of all twentieth-century castles are the two blocks of flats in Kingsbury, west London, designed by Ernest Trobridge in the 1930s: Rochester Court is faced with stone in imitation of Rochester Castle and Highfort Court has a crenellated roofline and tower.

In 1938 the architect Sir Basil Spence, best known for Knightsbridge Barracks and the rebuilding of the bomb-damaged Coventry Cathedral, built Broughton Place in the Scottish Borders, which is a modern interpretation of a traditional seventeenth-century tower house. Between 1946 and 1955 William Thomas built Easterheughs Castle, a conventional tower house overlooking the Firth of Forth in Fife on an outcrop of rock he had spotted while on fire watch over the coast in the Second World War as a member of the Home Guard. These are just a few of the new castles built in Scotland.

After the Second World War British country house and castle owners lost their confidence and the outlook for their survival was bleak. Consequently during the 1950s hundreds of houses and castles were demolished. W. Douglas Simpson, writing in 1957, encapsulated the pervading feeling amongst the landed classes: 'It is safe to prophesy that no more castles will be restored, and no new castles built by private money,

LEFT 23 Kensington Place,
London, an urban tower house
designed by Tom Kay, 1964–7.

RIGHT Corrour Lodge,
designed by Moshe Safdie
(1999–2003), stands at the
head of Loch Ossian in the
west Highlands.

in Britain ever again. It is clear that the day of the castle as a residence is over.'[37] How wrong he was! Castles continued to be built, and sixty years after these words were written the cult of the castle shows no sign of abating

One of the most imaginative examples is a modest town house, 23 Kensington Place in London, designed by architect Tom Kay in 1964–7. Slotted into a small-scale London streetscape, in profile it is an exciting composition of geometric shapes pierced by a tower, evoking the silhouette of a castle.

A more traditional approach is that employed at the end of the twentieth century by a dentist, John Mew, and his wife, who built Braylsham Castle, a diminutive castle deep in the Sussex Weald that appears to be the result of an accumulation of historical layers (see page 172).

In Scotland the celebrated Scottish architect Lachlan Stewart not only lives in a castle he restored but is in the midst of designing castle-inspired country houses. Scottish architect Ian Begg built for himself at Plockton near the Kyle of Lochalsh in 1987–9 a tower house with concrete walls, underfloor heating and even a lift shaft for his own use and an

Italianate loggia, perhaps inspired by the one at Dunderave. Corrour is a thrillingly brave modern interpretation of a Scottish castle in the midst of a 65,000-acre/26,304-hectare estate, designed by a Boston-based architect, Moshe Safdie (see page 184).

And Quinlan Terry, a contemporary architect best known for his classical country houses, designed Fort Brecqhou, a castle on the Isle of Sark, for the reclusive Barclay brothers, owners of the *Daily Telegraph*.

One of the great planning causes célèbres of the early twenty-first century, attracting the newspaper headline 'An Englishman's home is his castle', concerns a new castle hidden behind bales of hay in Surrey. The owner, a farmer, John Fidler, did not get planning permission, believing that he would not need it if he could prove that it had been standing for five years. The castle was ingeniously constructed by cladding two grain towers linked together by a brick structure which incorporates various salvaged architectural fragments. When he is not in Surrey, John Fidler lives in an old British fort on the coast in Ghana.

The castles explored in this book are wide-ranging in scope, from those restored by industrial tycoons and castle-collectors to restorations and new-builds by architects. Some such as Castle Drogo are monumental in scale; others such as Braylsham are modest. Uniting them all is a love of what has evolved over the centuries to be regarded as a very British type of structure. The majority of restorations discussed in this book are driven not by paintstaking historicisim, but more by a love of the romance a castle symbolizes. To want to live in a castle one has to be imbued with a powerful sense of history and place. Several of the owners, such as Claude Lowther, derived enormous pleasure in buying armour, antique furniture and paintings, and in the case of William Waldorf Astor antique statuary, to cater to this romantic sense of history. Each castle illustrated has its own unique story. All of them will no doubt continue to fascinate architectural historians for years to come as well as inspire yet more restorations and new designs.

NOTES

PAGE 4

1 William Allingham, *Flower Pieces and Other Poems*, Reeves & Turner, 1888

INTRODUCTION

2 John Goodall, *The English Castle,* Yale University Press, 2011

3 Adam Nicolson, *Sissinghurst: An Unfinished History,* Harper Press, 2008, p. 274

4 John Goodall, *The English Castle,* Yale University Press, 2011

5 Robert Liddiard, *Castles in Context: Power, Symbolism and Landscape 1066–1500*, Windgather Press, 2005

6 T.M. Devine, *The Scottish Nation*, Penguin, 1999

7 John Goodall, *The English Castle*, Yale University Press, 2011, p. 317

8 Ibid., p. 490

9 Ibid.

10 Stephen Astley, *Robert Adam's Castles,* Soane Museum, 2000, p. 15

11 Ibid., p. 15.

12 J. Mordaunt Crook, *William Burges and the High Victorian Dream,* John Murray, 1981, p. 259

13 H.V. Morton, *I Saw Two Englands: A Record of a Journey Before the War and After the Outbreak of the War in the Year 1939*, Methuen & Co., 1942, p. 121

14 Jeremy Musson, 'To Me the Past is Sacred', *Country Life*, 8 January 1998, p. 34

15 Kenneth Rose, *Superior Person: A Portrait of Curzon and his Circle in Late Victorian England*, Weidenfeld and Nicolson, 1969, p. 7

16 Lord Curzon's will

17 Jeremy Musson, 'To Me the Past is Sacred', *Country Life*, 8 January 1998, p. 34

18 Ibid.

19 *Bodiam Castle*, National Trust guidebook by David Thackray, 2003

20 *The Times*, 4 February 1926

21 Marchioness of Curzon, *Reminiscences*, Hutchinson, 1955, p. 56

22 Ibid.

23 *Bodiam Castle*, National Trust guidebook by David Thackray, 2003

24 Queen Elizabeth in conversation with Eric Anderson, 1994, in William Shawcross, *Queen Elizabeth The Queen Mother*, Macmillan, 2009

25 Letter from Commander Vyner to Queen Elizabeth, 23 August 1952, in William Shawcross, *Queen Elizabeth The Queen Mother*, Macmillan, 2009

26 Ibid.

27 Letter from Queen Elizabeth to Lady Katherine Farrell, 15 August 1979, Farrell Papers, William Shawcross, *Queen Elizabeth The Queen Mother*, Macmillan, 2009

28 A. Rowan and D. Walker, 'New Castles for Old: The Restorations of Tower Houses in Scotland 1', *Country Life*, 14 February 1974

29 Margherita Howard de Walden, *Pages from My Life*, Sidgwick and Jackson, 1965, p. 86

30 P.H. Ditchfield, *The Old English Squire*, Methuen & Co, 1912, p. 1

31 P.H. Ditchfield, *Vanishing England*, Methuen, 1911, p. 5

32 Vita Sackville-West, *The Heir*, William Heinemann, 1922

33 Lord Conway's diary, 10 March 1911

34 *The Cowdray Sale*, 13, 14 and 15 September 2011, Christie's, p. 12

35 M.E.M. Donaldson, *Wanderings in the Western Highlands and Islands*, A. Gardner, 1923, pp. 193–5

36 In conversation with Amicia de Moubray in June 2011

37 W. Douglas Simpson, *Exploring Castles*, Routledge & Kegan Paul, 1957, p. 157

LEFT Castle Drogo,
designed by Sir Edwin
Lutyens for Julius Drewe.

BAMBURGH CASTLE

NORTHUMBERLAND

'The whole of the new building is neither fish, flesh, fowl nor good red herring . . . It is only worth mentioning as exhibiting the acme of expenditure with the nadir of intelligent achievement,' wrote H. Avray Tipping in 1908.[38] Describing the restoration of Bamburgh Castle by Lord Armstrong, these were brutal words from *Country Life*'s leading architectural writer. Tipping was fulminating because Armstrong had not followed the castle's original plan and had instead extensively rebuilt it as a late Victorian country house masquerading as a medieval castle.

Tipping did not mention the astonishing fact that Lord Armstrong, the great Tyneside industrialist who had made a fortune principally from the sale of armaments, had embarked on such a daunting project at the advanced age of eighty-three. Like so many titans of the Victorian age, Lord Armstrong was prodigiously energetic and determined in every sphere of his long life.

Armstrong was born in 1810 in Newcastle, at the time a hotbed of intellectual fervour centred on the Lit and Phil Club, founded a few years earlier in 1802. Elected a Fellow of the Royal Society at the age of thirty-five, in the same year he demonstrated a model of his hydraulic crane at a meeting of the Lit and Phil. His cranes were the foundation of his works at Elswick, which he established two years later in 1847. The Swing Bridge in Newcastle to this day uses the hydraulic machinery Armstrong installed, as does London's Tower Bridge. By the time of his death in 1900, the Elswick works had grown into a global empire employing nearly 25,000 people.

Bamburgh is one of the great iconic images of Northumberland and occupies one of the most romantic sites of any English castle. It is built on a rocky promontory overlooking a sandy beach and its majestic, brooding silhouette rises out of a ravishing stretch of coast. Viewed from the south, its long façade is reminiscent of that of an Indian hill fort.

Originally built by the Normans, the castle was besieged by William II while it was owned by Robert de Moubray, Earl of Northumbria.[39] After he was taken prisoner, his wife conceded to the King only when he threatened to blind her husband. The castle then became a property of the English Crown. It was extensively damaged during the Wars of the Roses in the fifteenth century. In 1464 it became the first castle to capitulate to artillery when it was attacked by the Yorkist army of Edward IV.

James I installed Claudius Forster of a local Northumbrian family as royal constable and for the following century the family served as successive governors of the castle until eventually the Crown granted them ownership. The

LEFT Bamburgh Castle, Northumberland, one of the great medieval fortresses of the Scottish border, was remodelled by C.J. Ferguson between 1894 and 1906 for Lord Armstrong.

ABOVE Lord Armstrong, 1810–1900, the great Northumbrian armaments manufacturer.

RIGHT Bamburgh Castle's site
is among the most romantic of
any English castle.

LEFT C.J. Ferguson's muscular
approach to altering a medieval
castle can be clearly seen in this
detail of the staircase hall in the
Crewe Lodgings.

BELOW The inner ward
of Bamburgh Castle during
reconstruction.

last such governor was Sir William Forster, who died bankrupt in 1700. His brother-in-law, Lord Crewe, Bishop of Durham, bought his estates, which included Bamburgh. By this date the castle was a 'mere ruin almost buried in sand'.[40]

Despite extensive works undertaken by the Crewe trustees in the eighteenth century, when it was converted into a school and hospital, the castle was never fully repaired. When the news leaked out in 1893 that the Crewe trustees might put the castle up for auction, inevitably there was public suspicion. Whatever would happen, the *Newcastle Weekly Courant* wondered, if the highest bidder proved to be a 'speculative builder or an adventurous hotel-keeper'?[41] Armstrong, however, privately reassured the doubters that he would restore what H. Avray Tipping described as 'the ancient grandeur'[42] of the castle. He was, his biographer Henrietta Heald writes, 'keenly aware of the historical significance of Bamburgh, whose outstanding site and location – . . . some

50 miles north of Newcastle and 20 miles south of Berwick – had made it a natural fortress from earliest times'.[43] In an astute move he approached the trustees of the Crewe family's charitable trust and pre-empted a public auction. He won the trustees over by promising the use of two bedrooms in case any of them wanted to stay the night at Bamburgh, and the safekeeping of their library, pictures and other treasures.

He also stated that he had family connections with the castle through the family of his late sister's husband, William Watson. Watson on his mother's side was descended from the Greys of Shoreston, a settlement that had long formed part of the royal demesne of Bamburgh Castle. 'To Armstrong, Bamburgh Castle felt in a peculiar way like coming home,'[44] writes Henrietta Heald.

Lord Armstrong and his wife of nearly sixty years, Meggie, were childless. With Armstrong's encouragement, his great-nephew Willie Watson, who would be his heir, changed his name

BELOW The Captain's
Lodging staircase hall,
designed by C.J. Ferguson.

by royal licence to Watson-Armstrong, 'thus acknowledging', as Heald says, 'his destiny and blurring his line of descent'.[45] Three years after his great-uncle's death, Watson-Armstrong was created Lord Armstrong (of the second creation) of Bamburgh and Cragside.

Meggie had died just a few months before Armstrong approached the trustees. It would have been one of the last ventures he discussed with her and it may have been in part to assuage his grief that he threw himself into the rebuilding of Bamburgh. Work was virtually complete on Cragside, his great country house designed by Norman Shaw, 20 miles/ 32 kilometres to the south-west near Rothbury; perhaps he wanted another large-scale building venture and the prospect of owning Bamburgh – which he must have known all his life – was too exciting to pass by. At the time of his purchase the estate also included several hundred acres of land, including three farms, as well as a share in the Farne Islands.

In the Armstrong archive at Bamburgh there is a letter dated 24 April 1894 from Lord Armstrong to Lord Carlisle, the owner of Naworth Castle in Cumberland, who had recently employed the Carlisle-based architect Charles Ferguson. On black-rimmed mourning paper marked 'Draft', Armstrong sought Carlisle's advice on the choice of an architect to work on Bamburgh. 'The architect should be a man of good taste and some experience in archaeological work. I understand you employed Mr. Ferguson for restorations at Naworth. Will you tell me in strict confidence whether you think him qualified to undertake this work. I feel considerable responsibility in making this appointment.' In detail, he continued, 'the hall should only be part of the entire work but the rest should be more utilitarian than aesthetic. It will mainly consist of the adaption and enlargement of the existing building for a convalescent hospital suitable for the deserving poor.' He envisaged the hall would be used for 'exercise and recreation in bad weather. It will also be at the service of the Public for legitimate purposes and under proper restrictions.'[46]

It is conceivable that Armstrong's well-intentioned but eccentric idea of using Bamburgh as a genteel convalescent home was inspired by the example of an eighteenth-century Crewe trustee, Dr John Sharp. An antiquarian and an archdeacon of Northumberland, Sharp had devoted thirty-five years to restoring Bamburgh's monumental twelfth-century keep for the use of his family, but he also left part of it free to provide beds for up to thirty-five shipwrecked sailors.

As well as overseeing the project Ferguson, who had a passion for antiquarianism, was to play an influential role in buying pictures, furniture and works of art from London

RIGHT The hammerbeam
ceiling of the King's Hall,
made using teak from
Siam (now Thailand) and
modelled on St George's
Hall, Windsor Castle.

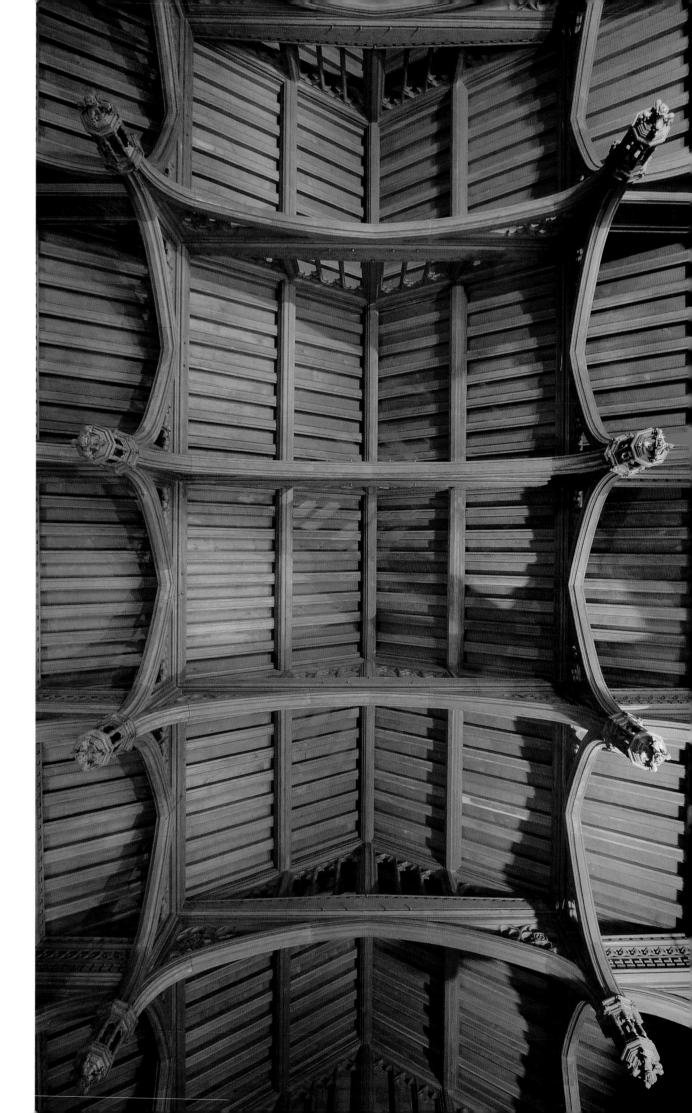

dealers for the castle's interiors. After his death, a Mr Hart, who seems to have been the clerk of works, wrote to Mrs Ferguson, 'Bamburgh was Mr. Ferguson's lifework, a part of himself and a long labour of love.'[47]

It took more than three years for the final plans to be drawn up. Their preparation culminated in a model of the proposed work being shown at the 1896 Royal Academy's Summer Exhibition and greeted with great excitement. The scale of the work was astounding. 'I should like 100 masons on the job in the summer months,' wrote Ferguson to Armstrong in May 1895. 'It is a great problem as to how to get sufficient masons in a country place, a problem that arises in every big undertaking. Skilled masons will not walk to and from a job if they can get work elsewhere without walking.'[48] Armstrong overcame this obstacle by erecting twenty or so timber-framed cottages for the workmen in the village of Bamburgh, and arranging a daily bus to and from the building site.

All manner of up-to-date technology was much in evidence, including a lift worked by hydraulic pressure in the medieval well shaft of the keep, gas and dynamo houses, and a complex water supply, which brought water from a source 5 miles/ 8 kilometres away by gravity.

As the century drew to a close it became increasingly obvious, from Armstrong's correspondence with his great-nephew William Watson-Armstrong, that the castle was destined to be the latter's home, not a place of repose for genteel convalescents. Drawings dated 1896 of the refectory, reading room and writing room intended for the hostel were all annotated, and these rooms became a library, an estate office and a business room. Armstrong retained a keen interest until the end of his life – in January 1899, for example, models of the pendants for the King's Hall were sent to him at Cragside. By the time of his death in December 1900 the majority of the construction work had been done; the decoration, both in the keep and in the main part of the castle, continued until 1902.

The King's Hall, a vast room built completely from scratch, has the heavy masculine clubbable atmosphere redolent of many typical interiors created by late Victorian and early Edwardian plutocrats. The hall has sombre teak panelling – exotically sourced from Siam (now called Thailand) – and teak was also used for the hammerbeam ceiling, which was modelled on that of St George's Hall, Windsor Castle. The furnishings comprise solid furniture upholstered in leather, large tapestries judiciously hung, a few paintings depicting only men, a scattering of oriental porcelain and a minstrels' gallery with a stained-glass window featuring many of the characters linked with the castle's history.

After Lord Armstrong's death William Watson-Armstrong inherited the castle. His son, the 3rd Lord Armstrong, died without issue and the castle is now owned by his two adopted children. It is partially divided into flats and the remainder is open to the public.

Avray Tipping's condemnation notwithstanding, the ambition of Lord Armstrong's rebuilding of an ancient castle in his dotage makes for a thrilling end to his remarkable life. The lavish restoration provides a fascinating contrast with Lutyens's very different approach at neighbouring Lindisfarne Castle (see page 62) a decade later. While Hudson's restoration was subtle and sophisticated, rejoicing in its simplicity and honesty to materials, Armstrong's taste was more in keeping with the opulence of a transatlantic nineteenth-century nouveau riche millionaire.

NOTES

BAMBURGH CASTLE

38 H. Avray Tipping, *Country Life*, 1908

39 Brother of my direct ancestor and namesake, Amicia de Moubray

40 Henrietta Heald, *William Armstrong: Magician of the North*, Northumbria Press, 2010 p. 228

41 Ibid., p. 231

42 Brochure for the Bamburgh Bazaar, held in aid of the Soldiers' & Sailors' Families Association at Bamburgh Castle, August 1900

43 Henrietta Heald, *William Armstrong: Magician of the North*, Northumbria Press, 2010, p. 229

44 Ibid.

45 Ibid., p. 230

46 Lord Armstrong to Lord Carlisle, 24 April 1894, Armstrong archive held at Bamburgh

47 Giles Worsley, 'Bamburgh Castle', *Country Life*, 27 August 1992, p. 47

48 Letter in the Armstrong archive held at Bamburgh

LYMPNE CASTLE
KENT

'As we stand on the paved terrace in the shadow of the castle's western tower and look out over [Romney] marsh, we may perhaps steal Mr. Kipling's pregnant fancies and see Parnesius, the Centurion of the Thirtieth, standing down the hill by the camp of Portus Lemani and the Roman fleet riding at anchor where now grows the lush grass of the marshes.' Thus writes H.G. Wells in his novel *Kipps*,[49] referring to Kipling's description of Lympne in *Puck of Pook's Hill*: 'If we were Dan and Una, Lympne is just the place where Puck would meet us as we walk up the dusty road from Westenhanger Station to the castle, and more, we should agree with Tom Shoesmith that "the world's divided like into Europe, Ashy, Afriky, Ameriky, Australy an' Romney Marsh."'[50]

Lympne is one of the most spectacularly sited castles in Britain. It is perched on top of an escarpment sloping steeply away to the south with a panoramic, map-like view over Romney Marsh, the Martello towers that punctuate the shore of the English Channel and even as far as France on a clear day. 'One climbs the Keep, up a tortuous spiral of stone, worn low to the pitch of perforation, and

LEFT The fourteenth-century western tower at Lympne Castle, restored by Sir Robert Lorimer.

RIGHT View of Lympne Castle from the south-west with the western tower on the right.

there one is lifted to the centre of far more than a hemisphere of a view,' writes Wells.[51]

The castle and the adjacent parish church of St Stephen form a highly picturesque grouping. The oldest part of the Kentish ragstone castle, a square-tower-like structure, probably dates from the thirteenth century, but the majority of it dates from the fifteenth century. In the eleventh century Archbishop Lanfranc had given the church of Lympne and its possessions to the Archbishop of Canterbury. It remained an ecclesiastical property until the middle of the nineteenth century.

Just below the castle are the Roman remains of Studfall Castle, built to guard what was then the estuary of the River Limene and described in Pevsner's guide to *West Kent and the Weald* as 'one of the few ruins to retain a Victorian flavour – heaps of rubble framed with wild flowers, browsing cattle, and the hazy marsh in the background'.[52]

Francis Tennant purchased Lympne in 1906. Known as Frank, he was the second son of Sir Charles Tennant, the Glaswegian chemicals magnate, one of the six richest men in late nineteenth-century Europe, who had been largely responsible for bringing the industrial revolution to Scotland, founding the Tennant chemical works at St Rollox. The works chimney, known as 'Tennant's Stalk', was 435 feet/132.5 metres high, three times the height of Nelson's Column, and it dominated Victorian Glasgow.

A sensitive, cultivated character, Frank Tennant was described by his sister, Margot Asquith, as 'the artist among the boys . . . he was born with a perfect ear for music and eye for colour and could distinguish what was beautiful in everything he saw'.[53] Despite being a second son, he was enormously wealthy. 'I am very, very happy,'[54] he telegraphed his wife on the day of his father's funeral in 1906. His father had left him £1 million.

In acquiring Lympne, Tennant successfully outbid Edward Hudson, who, weary of the long journey to Lindisfarne (see page 62), had been casting around for something more readily accessible from London. Tennant was a passionate golfer and Lympne's proximity to a golf club almost certainly clinched the deal for him.

The castle was nearly beyond redemption. 'A year or two more of neglect and it would have collapsed into a heap of scattered rubble like its Roman neighbour down the hill,'[55] a *Country Life* article observed. The ground floor of the tower had been used as a dairy and its upper level as a granary, and what is now the garden had degenerated into a farmyard. Over the centuries it had been subjected to many insensitive alterations. For example, at some stage a floor had been inserted at the level of the window transoms in the Great Hall.

Tennant engaged the Scottish architect Sir Robert Lorimer, presumably because he was impressed by the work Lorimer had started for his father shortly before the latter's death: the remodelling (following a fire) of Glen in Peeblesshire,[56] a baronial house bristling with turrets. Lorimer, often referred to as the Scottish counterpart to Sir Edwin Lutyens, was greatly influenced by his boyhood recollections of Kellie Castle in Fife, which his father, James, Professor of Public and International Law at Edinburgh University, had sensitively repaired as a summer dwelling. He had taken a lease of the ruined castle from the Earl of Mar and Kellie after discovering it in 1876. 'There was no wholesale gutting out, every bit of antiquity was preserved with loving care.'[57]

Robert Lorimer was a wise choice for Lympne, as he had an innate understanding of the different components that are so pleasing in such an assemblage of historic buildings. He had already demonstrated his sensitivity to the past by skilfully incorporating many elements of the late sixteenth- and early seventeenth-century architecture of Kellie in his designs for large country houses such as Formakin in Renfrewshire and for his restoration of Earlshall, a tower house near Kellie. Earlshall made Lorimer's name and it became well known through photographs that appeared in *Country Life*.

Lorimer was unusual amongst Scottish architects in having a significant English practice without ever opening a London office. For him Lympne was 'a most attractive job. I rather like

BELOW The north range of
Lympne Castle, encompassing
the servants' quarters designed
by Sir Robert Lorimer in a
gentle romantic manner.

a job south of London which takes you up every eight weeks or so in a sleeper at someone else's expense, and one is able to keep in touch with what is going on.'[58]

Lorimer's aim at Lympne was to allow the old castle to tell its own story, restoring it as far as possible to its original condition, so that both its internal arrangement and its general character might once more be seen. His plans differed from those drawn up by Lutyens, whom rashly Hudson had instructed before he had completed his proposed purchase. 'Sir Edwin tells me that his plans were much more formal and more in the style of semi-fortified Tudor buildings than

the essentially domestic type adopted by Lorimer,' writes Christopher Hussey.[59]

It was a challenging project, as the limitations imposed by the site were considerable. To the east the castle is bounded by the churchyard wall, and to the south the ground falls away sharply to the marshes. The road to the church from the village defines the northern boundary, and to the west the space available was limited. In addition, so precarious was the state of the castle that a major worry underlying the renovation was that the slightest alteration might result in the whole edifice tumbling down.

The initial impression of Lympne is of a cluster of buildings resembling a small tight-knit village, entered through an impressive archway with massive oak gates nearly 14 feet/4.25 metres high. On a windy day it would have been impossible to open them by hand, so gearing had to be installed, worked by a wheel in the gatehouse. The detached north range of servants' quarters has a soft picturesque air, enhanced by the dovecote and a round tower with a conical roof, perhaps evoking the vernacular idiom of local Kentish oast houses.

Lorimer was careful not to obliterate the ancient core, canted on the fifteenth-century hall, and discreetly added a new wing on to one side, joining the two with a corridor, as he had already done at Brackenbrough, Cumberland, and was to do later at Balmanno, Perthshire. He articulated the whole with tall, almost Mannerist, chimney stacks, which add a quirky note to what could be called a mellow manor-house effect. On the south side Lorimer accentuated the castle effect by restoring the west tower, which, backed by the solid mass of the great hall, stands out heroically on the terrace with its stone abutment, while the new wing, with its smaller scale and more broken outline, is not nearly so dominant. To take advantage of the spectacular views the dining room is canted on the axial line of the old castle, with a windowed bay looking out. This was the scene of a commotion in 1909 when the Prime Minister, Herbert Asquith, with his wife, Margot, Tennant's sister, was on holiday at Lympne. The dining room was stormed by suffragettes, who had tracked down the Prime Minister and hurled stones through the dining-room window.

There is a pleasing, understated Arts and Crafts simplicity to the interiors, with little inglenook seats and built-in shelves for displays of the then voguish collections of blue and white china. The ironwork executed by Thomas Hadden is particularly fine – for example, the grilles hiding the recessed radiators and the door handles and hinges. The furniture was a rich assortment of fifteenth-, sixteenth- and seventeenth-century oak tables, chairs and cabinets, and there were also fine Burgundian tapestries and Persian carpets. Possibly the most fascinating item, which has long since been lost, was a Steinway piano commissioned for the great hall by Tennant. It was painted by Phoebe Traquiar,[60] the painter and enamellist, with nine panels depicting the Song of Solomon against a background of Scottish scenery. The Tennants lost a son in the Great War in 1916 and put the castle up for sale the next year. In 1919 it was bought by Henry Beecham, brother of the conductor, Sir Thomas Beecham, both of them grandsons of Thomas Beecham, the inventor of Beecham's pills.

When the castle came on the market again in 1932 Knight, Frank and Rutley's sales particulars describe Lympne as 'an ancient fortified residence that has retained essentially its original appearance, but whose grim character and purpose have been mellowed by passing centuries into a quiet dignity, so that with careful restoration and modernization of the interior arrangements and equipment it now combines the rare quality of medieval charm with modern comfort and luxury'. The sales particulars illustrate an unusual feature, a covered tennis court with a small spectators' gallery lit by electricity. The castle has subsequently changed hands several times. In 1960 it was bought along with 200 acres/81 hectares for £40,000 by Harry Margary, newly wealthy after selling the garden of his home in Bagshot, Surrey, to a property developer. His son, Aubyn, who added a 'de' to his surname, was a founder member of the 20th Century Fops Association, a group of modern-day Beau Brummels who paraded around London in Regency dress in the 1960s. The castle was last sold in 1999 and is now available for hire for weddings and corporate events.

LEFT Lorimer's sensitive restoration is apparent in the pleasingly simple staircase landing.

ABOVE RIGHT A collection of voguish blue and white china arranged on built-in display shelves.

NOTES

LYMPNE CASTLE

49 H.G. Wells, *Kipps: The Story of a Simple Soul*, Macmillan, 1905

50 Rudyard Kipling, *Puck of Pook's Hill*, Macmillan, 1906, a story told to two children living in Pevensey by people magically plucked out of history by Puck, who refers to himself as 'the oldest thing in England'

51 H.G. Wells, *Kipps: The Story of a Simple Soul*, Macmillan, 1905

52 John Newman, *West Kent and The Weald* (Pevsner Architectural Guides: Buildings of England), Penguin, 1969, p. 394

53 *The Autobiography of Margot Asquith*, Thornton Butterworth, 1920, p. 4

54 Simon Blow, *Broken Blood: The Rise and Fall of the Tennant Family*, Faber & Faber, 1987, p. 120

55 *Country Life*, 12 November 1910, p. 685

56 Glen, originally designed by David Bryce in 1853 for Sir Charles Tennant (Frank Tennant's father) and altered 1905–7 by Lorimer, who was also responsible for a lodge, a walled garden and stables.

57 Louise Lorimer (daughter of Professor James Lorimer), *Kellie Castle and Garden* (guidebook), National Trust for Scotland

58 Peter Savage, *Lorimer and the Edinburgh Craft Designers*, Harris, 1980

59 Christopher Hussey, *The Work of Sir Robert Lorimer*, Country Life, 1931

60 Phoebe Traquair (1852–1936), an Irish-born artist, who moved to Edinburgh in 1874 after marrying the Scottish palaeontologist Ramsay Heatley Traquair. She was an important figure in the Scottish Arts and Crafts movement.

HEVER CASTLE
KENT

Of all the slumbering decaying castles whose resurrection was bankrolled by American money, Hever Castle is the most extraordinary for the staggering scale of its transformation.

It is not recorded why William Waldorf Astor came to buy Hever in 1903, but his love of history and his passion for the occult were probably both important factors. Like many other wealthy men he collected houses: he owned a house in Carlton House Terrace in London; a house in Brighton; Cliveden, an estate in Berkshire on the Thames, which he bought from the Duke of Westminster; and a villa near Sorrento on the Amalfi coast in Italy.

The compact moated castle, dating in parts from 1270, was the childhood home of Anne Boleyn. There is an unsubstantiated story that the ghost of the unhappy queen roams through the castle and on stormy nights, in a dark panelled chamber where Henry VIII had trysts with his bride, mournful love songs can be heard. Astor, keen to verify this tale, asked the Psychical Research Society to keep watch during Christmas over the course of several years, but to no avail.

On his father's death in 1890, Astor became the richest man in New York, with an income of $6–9 million a year from rents on his properties. The next year, following a feud over matters of social seniority with his aunt, Caroline Webster Schermerhorn Astor, he moved with his family to England, declaring, much to the wrath of his fellow countrymen, 'America is good enough for any man who has to make a livelihood, though why travelled people of independent means should remain there more than a week is not readily to be comprehended.'[61] He became a British subject in 1899.

Lonely, shy, odd, reclusive, secretive, complex, Astor was – unlike other members of his family – also a sensitive aesthete, devoted to collecting works of art, rather than a shrewd businessman. When at the age of eighteen he had been introduced by his German tutor to Greek philosophy, the experience was one that he later compared to the conversion of St Paul. In 1880 he was appointed American minister in Rome, where he filled his days pursuing 'archaeology, pictures, Renaissance history, and excursions in the thrill and glory of the Campagna'.[62]

For much of the nineteenth century Hever had been occupied by tenant farmers. Inevitably it had been allowed to decay; some rooms were partitioned, some of the oak panelling whitewashed and the grounds neglected, even though it was occasionally open to the public. In 1895 Captain Guy Sebright took a lease on the castle and set about renovating it with his wife, although

BELOW North-west aspect of
Hever Castle, with the outer
moat in the foreground.

it is questionable how sympathetic his vision was – *Country Life* describes him as 'a gentleman of restoring proclivities, of whom we will say nothing further than that he pulled down the very interesting Tudor stabling . . . in order to get old timber for his work'.[63]

Astor lavished prodigious sums of money on Hever, turning the estate into an opulent Edwardian fantasy more in the spirit of the great Vanderbilt palaces on Rhode Island than of rural west Kent.

A large part of the castle's charm is its pleasing compact, jewel-like quality, but this meant that the castle was far too small to accommodate sumptuous Edwardian country house weekends and the requisite staff. Astor's architect was Frank Loughborough Pearson (son of John Loughborough Pearson, who had designed the Astor estate office in Temple Gardens in London, overlooking the Thames). He brilliantly solved the problem of size by designing a 100-room irregular cluster of offices and guest cottages, on the other side of the moat (roughly in the shape of a square courtyard with a couple of offsets to the north), resembling a rambling Tudor village such as might have nestled beneath the walls of an ancient castle. The village was connected to the castle by a covered bridge across the moat.

Drawing heavily on the Kentish vernacular architectural style, Loughborough Pearson's scheme is an extremely successful medley of what appear to be several different cottages haphazardly grouped together. Constructed of a variety of materials – some are tile hung, some half-timbered – they create the illusion of a village that has evolved over time. In the spirit of the pretence, different parts of this village have romanticized folksy names such as Medley Cottage, the Smuggler's Room and Orchard Cottage. 'For a moment I could not believe', said Astor, 'they had been built a few short months ago, they seemed so old and crooked.'[64]

The village included offices, kitchens and staff quarters, as well as twenty-five guest bedrooms. The basement was a vast warren of passages connecting the various domestic offices,

clad in practical glazed white tiles. No guest, once indoors, could imagine himself in anything but a vast sprawling country house, albeit one that was hard to navigate. 'The result is somewhat bewildering within, and the newly-arrived guest may well need the help of numerous arrows and notices abounded throughout the corridors and halls to his allotted quarters,'[65] commented *Country Life*.

By December 1904 748 workmen were engaged upon the castle, village and pleasure grounds. They received a Christmas present of 2lb of beef each, a slice of cake, and threepence worth of tobacco, at a cost of two shillings a head. Some of the workmen and their families were put up in a temporary hutment on site. All the available lodgings in the neighbouring towns and villages were taken. Some men walked 7 miles/11 kilometres daily from Westerham, while others were brought by special train from London each day. One man had the sole job of carting 45 gallons/205 litres of beer every day for their consumption.

Astor, who lived in constant fear of assassination, went to extraordinary lengths to keep curious snoopers out while the work was carried out. No workmen could enter without a special pass and nobody was allowed to take a photograph. Eight private detectives worked in relays throughout the day and four by night. It was sometimes said that his middle name was 'Walled-off'.

Wisely, Astor and Loughborough Pearson left the exterior of the old castle alone, except for making some vital repairs to the stonework, but little remained of the interior. This allowed them the freedom to create a superb sequence of rooms, which formed a backdrop to Astor's outstanding collection of antique furniture, objects and ornaments. Philip Tilden described Hever as 'a miniature Metropolitan Museum of New York'.[66]

Astor was adamant that all the work should be undertaken strictly in the spirit of the past, adhering as much as possible to traditional sixteenth-century techniques. For example, the use of planes to make the panelling for the dining hall was

BELOW The sprawling 100-room
'medieval' village designed by Frank
Loughbrough Pearson to provide
the necessary extra rooms for an
Edwardian millionaire's country
house dominates the compact castle
when viewed from above.

LEFT Top left: Staff of engineers, electricians and maintenance men in 1907. Top right: A pair of housemaids in 1907. Below: A team of ten men and four horses transporting a Scots pine from Ashdown Forest to Hever in 1907.

BELOW Craftsmen in the studio of W.S. Frith. The panelling of South American sabicu was cut and carved in London, and brought by train to Hever in completely finished sections, ready to install.

prohibited; everything had to be executed using the adze and the chisel. Avray Tipping was complimentary about the standard of craftsmanship, writing in *Country Life*: 'We have come across no other examples of these reproduced Jacobean ceilings where the old feeling and the old surface have been obtained to anything like the extent we find at Hever in several rooms. The attempt is most praiseworthy.' Wherever possible doors, locks, windows and glass were replaced with the best materials in the manner of the sixteenth century, again winning the praise of Avray Tipping: 'Mr. Pearson has induced the modern workman to lay aside the mechanical finish so dear to him, and leave some mark of the tool and hand . . . the result is most satisfying.'[67]

When it came to designing the new rooms Pearson and Astor drew on many historic examples. The old kitchen, for instance, was converted into a staircase hall with richly carved columns of Italian walnut and a gallery and staircase inspired by the screen of King's College Chapel, Cambridge, and carved by W.S. Frith. Astor's keen interest in the paranormal may explain why the oak panelling in the drawing room, inlaid with bog oak and holly, was a copy of that in the inlaid room at Sizergh Castle in Cumbria (which had recently been sold to the Victoria and Albert Museum), well known for the screaming lady ghost who haunted it. In the west wing the library and the study are lined with panelling and bookcases of sabicu, a naturally scented wood which is as hard as ebony, from South America. The design of the bookcases was inspired by those once owned by Samuel Pepys, now at Magdalene College, Cambridge, and the ceiling of the library is copied from one at Hampton Court Palace. The floor is made of Spanish mahogany laid on Swedish pine.

Perhaps even more astonishing than Astor's alterations to the castle were the 125-acre/50-hectare pleasure gardens. These included a 38-acre/15-hectare man-made lake, avenues, walks, shrubberies, herbaceous borders, woodland gardens, a maze and chessmen in clipped golden yew based on Tudor examples Astor had seen in the British Museum. They were laid out between 1904 and 1908 by Joseph Cheal and Son with more than a thousand men. Pearson was responsible for the design of the formal Italian garden with its stone walls, rotundas, loggia, piazza and pergola. Cheal's designed the Roman Bath, the Blue Corner, the Cascade Rockeries and the 240-foot/73-metre long Gallery of Grottoes. An extensive network of railways and a fleet of steam diggers were used to make the new features and contours.

Over the years Astor had accumulated an outstanding collection of antique statuary, including sculpted wellheads,

LEFT William Waldorf Astor described 'Tudor' houses as 'possessing such individuality as though they had grown up one by one in various ages'. Top left: New guest rooms beyond the north moat. Bottom left: The office courtyard. Top right: The covered bridge linking the new village to the castle. Bottom right: A guest house.

LEFT The hall
and gallery,
photographed in
1907 for *Country
Life*.

RIGHT Detail of
the panelling in
the drawing room,
made from oak, bog
oak and holly, and
inspired by panelling
at Sizergh Castle,
Cumbria.

FOLLOWING
PAGES The loggia
and piazza in the
Italian garden.

columns of porphyry, figures of gods and goddesses, winged beasts and sarcophagi, several of which he had bought during his time in Rome. These were shipped from Rome and assembled in a long corrugated iron shed by the castle before being placed in position in September 1907. He was still adding to his collection in 1913, despite observing: 'Over the past 40 years Italy has been picked clean as a bone of fine things.'[68] Interestingly he was in the vanguard of what would decades later become widespread conservation practice. He wrote to Lady Sackville in February 1913, 'There will not be much to see, for in winter, the marbles are all in waterproof jackets.'[69]

Not everyone agreed with Avray Tipping's view that Hever 'offers a most interesting exhibition of the extremely good results which the modern designer and the modern craftsmen, at their best, are able to achieve'.[70] Fleur Cowles in *The Astors* quotes one critic: 'I can hardly bear to tell of the things that this man did to Hever: the diverting of a river, the bringing of

fully grown trees and rocks to mask from public gaze a castle which was historic but long had been a farmhouse to which any courteous stranger might be admitted. He built onto it and altered it and had costly sham antiques made, and then enclosed the whole within high walls and huge electrically operated gates so that when his motor car came, the door opened silently and closed smoothly and swiftly almost upon the back of the car as it entered.'[71]

Astor's extraordinary vision for Hever came into its own when his son, John Jacob, who purchased *The Times* in 1922, began holding occasional parties at the castle exclusively for the *The Times* staff. These proved very popular and attracted a growing number of employees every time – there were more than four thousand on one memorable occasion. There must have been a wonderful *fête champêtre* atmosphere as thousands of employees arriving on special trains from London were royally entertained. There was a splendid array

LEFT View over the 38-acre lake from the loggia.

RIGHT The Nymphs Fountain, designed by W.S. Frith (1850–1924) in 1908, was inspired by the Trevi Fountain in Rome.

of activities on offer: a fleet of rowing boats on the lake invited the energetic to take exercise; among the younger visitors of both sexes some bathed in the lake, a few played tennis, and a great many took part in a treasure hunt that required an active mind and persistence. There were conducted tours of the castle, a flower show, a golf competition, a photographic competition and even dancing on the lawn to the band of the Royal Artillery.

In 1915, Astor was elevated to the peerage, taking the title Lord Astor of Hever. He died of heart failure at his home in Brighton in 1919. Surprisingly his ashes lie under the marble floor of the chapel at Cliveden, not at Hever.

In 1968 the castle suffered extensive flood damage when more than 5 inches/13 centimetres of rain fell in sixteen hours. Hever lies close to the River Eden, a tributary of the Medway. Water swamped the castle, several cottages and the stables to the extent that staff had to be dramatically evacuated by boat and lifeline. It took nearly two years for the rooms to dry out and many of the contents were ruined. The renovation work was only completed in 1972.

In 1946 the National Trust turned down Hever Castle as being a 'gross fake'.[72] Lord Astor's descendants stayed put for almost another forty years, finally selling it in 1983 to Broadland Properties, who open the castle and the grounds on a regular basis.

NOTES

HEVER CASTLE

61 Virginia Cowles, *The Astors*, Weidenfeld and Nicolson, 1979, p. 148

62 William Waldorf Astor, *Silhouettes*, privately printed, 1917

63 *Country Life*, 1917

64 Clive Aslet, *The Last Country Houses*, Yale University Press, 1982

65 H. Avray Tipping, 'Hever Castle', *Country Life*, 19 October 1907

66 Philip Tilden, *True Remembrances: The Memoirs of an Architect*, Country Life, 1954, p. 114

67 H. Avray Tipping, 'Hever Castle', *Country Life*, 19 October 1907

68 Letter from W.W. Astor to Lady Sackville, 4 May 1913, in the Nicolson Papers

69 Ibid., 4 February 1913

70 H. Avray Tipping, 'Hever Castle', *Country Life*, 19 October 1907

71 Virginia Cowles, *The Astors*, Weidenfeld and Nicolson, 1979

72 James Lees Milne, Diary, 9 January 1946

LINDISFARNE CASTLE
NORTHUMBERLAND

'Just got a telewire from Hudson saying he has got Lindisfarne Castle – I will go and look . . . It will be amusing,' was Edwin Lutyens's response on learning that Edward Hudson had purchased it in January 1902.[73]

Hudson, founder of *Country Life*, and Peter Anderson Graham, later editor of *Country Life* and author of *Highways and Byways in Northumbria*, discovered the derelict abandoned castle on Holy Island, off the Northumberland coast, while on holiday in 1901. Hudson was immediately captivated by it, and bought a lease from the Crown a few months later.

Glimpsed from the mainland the castle has an ethereal appearance, as if it is a mirage on the horizon. The approach to the island has an eerie feel, as one has to drive for what seems for ever through the dunes and across the causeway to reach it.

St Aidan had established a church on the island known as Lindisfarne in the seventh century ('farne' comes from the Celtic *fahren*, 'a place of retreat'). Aidan was succeeded in 685 by St Cuthbert, whose celebrated holy life, coupled with the discovery of his miraculously preserved body, inspired the creation of the illuminated manuscript known as the Lindisfarne Gospels. Benedictine monks from Durham built a monastery, which contains St Cuthbert's remains, on the island in the twelfth century. The monks christened Lindisfarne 'Holy Island' to commemorate St Cuthbert and it has been a place of pilgrimage ever since.

Following Henry VIII's dissolution of the monasteries, Lindisfarne, strategically well placed for quelling Border rebellions, was fortified by the English Crown in 1570–72. Over the next three centuries the fort's importance dwindled, until by the end of the nineteenth century it was being used only intermittently by the occasional coastguard.

Curiously, Charles Rennie Mackintosh had sketched the castle only six months before Hudson saw it. It bears an uncanny resemblance to the south façade of Glasgow School of Art, the first stage of which he had recently completed. Mackintosh's drawings celebrate the 'sublime monumentality of the faceted plans of tough stone wall rising from the rock, and these were the elements that inspired Lutyens in his restoration', writes Gavin Stamp.[74]

Hudson's brief to Lutyens was to transform the castle, then a ruin, into a holiday house with plenty of bedrooms for house parties during the summer months. Work began in 1903 and was completed in July 1906. More bedrooms were added in 1912. Lutyens's imaginative and sensitive scheme did little to alter the castle's rugged external appearance. He cleverly manipulated the

LEFT Lindisfarne Castle, viewed from the north-west.

ABOVE The sixteenth-century castle in a ruinous state before restoration by Sir Edwin Lutyens.

different levels both inside and outside. 'The route to and through the building is both external and internal, rising up ramps and stairs to reach a succession of terraces with new shapes and new spaces constantly becoming visible,' writes Gavin Stamp.[75] From the upper battery there is a superb prospect out over the sea along the coast to Bamburgh Castle with the Farne Islands in the distance.

As Christopher Hussey writes: 'The poetry of the building derives from the effects having been got almost entirely by structural means – walls, vaults, apertures and in the avoiding of all but the broadest suggestion of "period". Consequently there is no hint of faking and so of make belief: the new masonry is as generously devised as the old but its profiles are not copies, they are solutions attained by reviewing the old mason's traditions afresh: the romance is real.'[76]

Sir Lawrence Weaver, a regular contributor to *Country Life*, opined 'a rude blockhouse has become a home of reasonable comfort' and praised Hudson for not 'demanding that wealth of modern devices which some people insist on installing in the most ancient of fabrics'.[77] There was no electricity or gas; the only source of lighting was candles. It was a far cry from Lord Armstrong's Bamburgh Castle a few miles distant, which

was brimming with modern technology. As the castle was used only in the summer months when, being so far north, it enjoyed long hours of daylight, this was not a serious problem and must have greatly added to the atmosphere of the place.

Lytton Strachey was less impressed. He was spitefully rude about 'Huddy' (Hudson), despite accepting his generous hospitality, describing him as 'a pathetically dreary figure – so curiously repulsive, too, and so, somehow, lost . . . A kind of bourgeois gentilhomme also.' As for the castle, it was 'a poor affair – except for the situation, which is magnificent, and the great foundations and massive battlements, whence one has amazing prospects of sea, hills, other castles, etc – extraordinarily romantic – on every side. But the building itself is all timid Lutyens – very dark, with nowhere to sit, and nothing but stone under, over and round you which produces a distressing effect – especially when one's hurrying downstairs late for dinner – to slip would be instant death. No – not a comfortable place, by any means.'[78]

ABOVE Left: Studio portrait of Edward Hudson, founding publisher of *Country Life* and owner of Lindisfarne Castle. Right: Portrait of Sir Edwin Lutyens as Master of the Art Workers' Guild, 1933, by Meredith Frampton.

ABOVE Pencil sketch
by G.H. Kitchin of the
Country Life architectural
writer Avray Tipping,
sitting at a desk in
Lindisfarne Castle in 1907.

Surprisingly he does not mention the bathing arrangements, which he must have found trying. 'The one bath is in continual use. There is a notice over the bath stating that as water has to be pumped up 350ft by hand folks are begged not to take a bath more than 6" deep,' wrote Sir Martin Conway in a letter to his wife, describing a weekend house party in August 1908.[79]

But Hudson clearly revelled in living at Lindisfarne the rural idyll that he so successfully promoted through the pages of *Country Life*. 'I want to amuse myself with the place,' he said in 1902.[80] Certainly Conway enjoyed his weekend. 'We are a very merry party'; 'Hudson is as happy as a sandboy'; 'he is really very simple and nice in these surroundings'; 'The other folk go golfing, fishing etc.' Conway describes having tea on the sands – 'We made a fire and boiled the kettle and the golfers joined us and some bathed and some paddled, it was warm and delightful' – and continues, 'We play bridge in the evening. Our food is good but simple. Breakfast eggs, bacon and fish if they've caught any, lunch I forgot, dinner, soup,

meat, pudding, cheese, coffee, claret or whiskey or ginger-beer.' Conway's fellow houseguests were the Portuguese cellist Madame Guilhermina Suggia ('they are thicker than ever'), Mr and Mrs Fort (Mr Fort was a South African company director, a friend of Alfred Beit and Cecil Rhodes, founders of the De Beers diamond company), two ladies 'who do something with fashion' and John Colvin, 'the young leader writer on the Morning Post who is so highly thought of'.[81]

To those visitors more used to staying in opulent Edwardian country houses, Lindisfarne's austere interiors must have seemed strikingly original. Hudson adhered to the discriminating taste being advocated through the pages of his magazine, furnishing the castle with antique oak furniture of the sixteenth and seventeenth centuries and domestic objects of brass and pewter as well as a few pieces designed by Lutyens such as the oval dining-room table. The walls were whitewashed and the floors were either of bare bricks or oak floorboards painted duck-egg blue or crimson and finished with a thin coat of white paint. Pattern was restricted to the odd Persian carpet, blue and white china and a few floral curtains. It appears that Hudson did not want anything to distract the eye from the spectacular

scenery visible from every window and the outdoor pursuits on offer; it was enough to be on holiday residing in a rescued castle. The understated interiors are shown in photographs of Lutyens's daughter Barbara (Barbie) at Lindisfarne, taken by the *Country Life* photographer Charles Latham in the manner of seventeenth-century Dutch paintings, with echoes of Vermeer and de Hooch, during the summer of 1906. The Lutyens family were frequent summer guests, although Lady Emily was not enamoured by the castle, finding it uncomfortable and cold.

ABOVE Barbara Lutyens, one of the daughters of Sir Edwin Lutyens at Lindisfarne, in 1906, photographed by Charles Latham.

RIGHT A fireplace. Far right, above: A gallery stairway. Far right, below: The Ship Room.

PAGES 68–9
Lindisfarne Castle seen from the garden, which was specifically designed by Gertrude Jekyll to be in full flower during the summer months.

PAGES 70–71
Left: Dining room with simple brick floor and old English oak furniture. Right: The entrance hall to the kitchen.

LEFT The oval dining-room table Sir Edwin Lutyens designed for Lindisfarne.

OPPOSITE Lindisfarne Castle appears to grow organically out of a rocky outcrop.

Hudson's initial plans for the castle's surroundings were ambitious. They were more in keeping with a typical late nineteenth/early twentieth-century gentlemen's country seat, and included a walled croquet lawn and tennis court. He also planned two gatehouses as well as a new pier for mooring yachts. The cost of these was huge, and they were never built. But he turned to Gertrude Jekyll for a garden scheme sympathetic to his treatment of the castle. He also created a water garden in the boggy area immediately to the north of the castle, known as the Stank, with the aim of attracting birds.

In May 1906 Jekyll travelled by train to Lindisfarne, accompanied by Lutyens and a cantankerous raven called Black Jack. 'The raven was an awful anxiety on the journey and carrying her on my lap across the sands,' Lutyens wrote to his wife. Somewhat stout, Jekyll was gingerly helped into a small boat by Hudson's manservant and rowed over to Holy Island. 'Bumps is quite charmed and so appreciative,' wrote Lutyens.[82] Following Jekyll's instructions, flowering plants were picturesquely planted amongst the rocks beneath the castle in 1906 and 1908. But it was not until 1911 that Jekyll's main plan was implemented. This transformed what had previously been a small walled garden growing vegetables for the fort into a flower garden that was visible from the windows of the main bedrooms. It was designed to be in full bloom in June, July and August, when Hudson and his friends were in residence.

Surprisingly Hudson did not buy the freehold until 1918. He had intended to leave Lindisfarne to his godson, Bill Congreve, but Congreve was killed in the First World War, awarded a posthumous VC. So Hudson decided to sell only two years later. Knight Frank's sales particulars describe the rural idyll that Hudson and Lutyens between them had created out of the castle: '3 Golf courses, excellent yacht anchorage, fishing very fine wildfowl/shooting to be sold with its important collection of antique furniture mainly of the Carolean and Jacobean periods and exceptional collection of rare pewter, brass work and old engravings.'

A stockbroker, Oswald Falk, bought Lindisfarne and much of the contents for £25,000 in 1921, but after a few years sold it on to Sir Edward Stein, a merchant banker and a man of catholic tastes. Stein gave it to the National Trust in 1944 and remained as its tenant until his death in 1965.

NOTES

LINDISFARNE CASTLE

73 Letter from Sir Edwin Lutyens to his wife, Lady Emily Lutyens, 1 February 1902

74 Gavin Stamp, *Edwin Lutyens: Country Houses from the Archives of Country Life*, Aurum Press, 2001, p. 117

75 Ibid., p. 119

76 Christopher Hussey, *The Life of Sir Edwin Lutyens*, Country Life, 1953, p. 107

77 Lawrence Weaver, *Houses and Gardens by Edwin Lutyens*, Country Life, 1921, p. 39

78 Lytton Strachey's letter is among the Hutchinson Papers in the Harry Ransom Humanities Research Center, University of Texas at Austin, and is quoted in the National Trust guidebook to Lindisfarne

79 Letter from Sir Martin Conway to his wife, held in the Conway Papers, Cambridge University Library

80 Oliver Garnett, *Lindisfarne Castle*, The National Trust, 1999

81 Ibid.

82 Letter from Sir Edwin Lutyens to his wife, Lady Emily Lutyens, 12 May 1906

ALLINGTON CASTLE

KENT

LEFT Allington Castle.

ABOVE Steps from the privy
garden to the courtyard.

'Wanted to purchase, old manor-house or abbey, built in the sixteenth century or earlier, with old garden, not much land, no sporting facilities, preferably five miles or more from a railway station.' So read an advertisement placed in *The Times* by Sir Martin Conway on 15 May 1905.

Sir Martin Conway (1856–1937), later Baron Conway of Allington, was a polymath who crammed an astonishing amount into his life: he was an alpine mountaineer, the first director of the Imperial War Museum, a noted collector of Italian Old Masters, Slade Professor of Fine Art at Cambridge, the author of more than twenty books, a Unionist MP for the Combined Universities and, by donating his collection of 100,000 photographs of art and architecture, responsible for establishing the Conway Library at the Courtauld Institute. He was also relentlessly ambitious – tellingly he pasted into his diary a cartoon from *The Times* depicting him as 'The Climber' – and knew everybody, including the Duveens, the Melchetts, Percy Macquoid, Edmund Gosse, Henry James, Sir Edwin Lutyens and Edith Wharton. He retained his formidable energy into old age. At the age of seventy-three he thought nothing of walking from Menton to Monte Carlo and back.

Conway received two replies to his advertisement. One described what he dismissed as 'a real beast of a building' – a stuccoed 'castellated mansion, suitable for a hotel or a hydro';[83] but he was immediately bewitched by the other, which described 'a medieval castle in such fascinating detail that it seemed impossible to believe that a building so delightful could exist. It told of moats and towers, of two courtyards of high embattled walls, of dovecots, tilting yard and I know not what other high sounding reminiscences from the days of chivalry'.[84] 'So incredulous was I as to the existence of a castle at Allington . . . that I hardly thought a journey down into Kent worthwhile.' However, he and his wife did make the journey, and it proved to be a 'turning point in our lives, little as we expected any such result when we set off'.[85] Conway ecstatically describes their first sight of Allington: 'The beauty of it was overwhelming. It took our breath away and for the moment we were speechless. Then we both gasped out "of course we must have it."'[86] Being just outside Maidstone on the left bank of the River Medway, it had the added attraction of being less than 10 miles/16 kilometres from Conway's birthplace.

On discovering that the Kentish antiquarian Aymer Vallance[87] had offered Lord Romney[88] £4,750, Conway appealed to Manton Marble, his American stepfather-in-law, on 27 July. 'His [Vallance's] offer is to be accepted unless tomorrow I make the following offer . . . £4,800.' Happily for Conway, Marble

OPPOSITE View from the
north-east of the ivy-bedecked
castle before it was rescued.

LEFT The inner courtyard.

replied by telegram the same day, 'I will help tide you over if you make the offer.'[89]

The original castle on the site had been destroyed on the instructions of Henry II in 1174. It was replaced with a fortified manor house, which was considerably enlarged by the Lord Warden of the Cinque Ports, Stephen de Penchester, in 1281 after Edward I granted a licence to crenellate. The castle then descended through several generations of Cobhams. The Wyatt family bought it in 1492 and the rebel leader Thomas Wyatt was born there in 1521.

During the Wyatts' ownership the castle was badly damaged by fire in around 1600. For the next three hundred years, the remains were woefully neglected and occupied by a succession of farmers. In 1895 Dudley C. Falke, a London barrister, rented part of the ruins, imaginatively using the walls to grow roses and undertaking some minor repairs. He 'stepped in at a critical moment and saved the place from destruction'. Ten years before he had found it to be considered no longer fit even to house the two labourers' families that had succeeded the farmers who used to dwell in it. Alarmed by the tale of the neighbouring Leybourne Castle tumbling down a few years earlier as a result of being engulfed by rampant ivy, the Conways' first task on taking possession of Allington was to prevent a similar fate befalling it. 'It took several men some months to clear the ivy which had trunks as "thick as a strong man's thigh",' wrote Conway.[90]

Conway's diaries show him to be a man of a highly romantic disposition, recording numerous moonlight walks around the castle. Lady Conway was a romantic, too, and by all accounts rather strange. Molly, the Countess of Berkeley, describes her arriving at Berkeley Castle in Gloucestershire 'dressed in orange brocade, with a medieval pointed cap on her head from which floated a long veil . . . In the evening she came to dinner dressed in white and holding a Madonna lily.'[91] Lord Clark describes her as '[Lord Conway's] weird old wife'.[92]

At first the Conways disagreed on what to do with Allington. Conway, swept along by enthusiasm, wanted to make it their principal residence, but his wife took a more pragmatic line and 'was all for occupying the inhabited part as a weekend cottage'. She foresaw 'vistas of expensive and uncomfortable rebuilding'. Initially she had her way but Martin prevailed.[93] 'The more familiar we became with the building the more certain we grew that it should be made our home,' wrote Conway some years later in Country Life.

'Our restoration ideals grow in dimensions, complexity. The beauty and concurrence of it all are perfection . . . It is great fun to build castles,' enthused Katrina Conway shortly after she and her husband took possession.[94]

Conway's initial plan was to repair the medieval parts of the castle, making what had originally been the Tudor kitchen house habitable. He enlisted the architect W.D. Caroe, a noted antiquary and archaeologist, to oversee the works,

RIGHT A romantic view of the
Italianate garden designed by
Philip Tilden.

embarking on the restoration about a year after purchasing it. The Conways moved in the following autumn.

'The principles we laid down for our governance were these: to preserve and manifest every ancient feature; to follow the precedent set by previous owners during the last six centuries, viz., to retain perfect freedom to make new doors, windows and staircases, and the like features wherever they were needed, but in doing so to manifest their modern date,' wrote Conway.[95] The works began with the long gallery and continued around the courtyard to the west range and gatehouse. Caroe recreated the machicolations of the gatehouse and rebuilt the roofs, adding new windows, floors and fireplaces. Garderobes were converted into bathrooms for the five bedrooms. Battlements and arrow-shoots were copied from surviving examples. Conway was not afraid to use the latest modern building materials: the ground floors were damp-proofed with concrete and asphalt and steel girders were used for beams.

In retrospect Caroe was to regret not tackling the great hall first, but understandably he had felt nervous about starting with such an immense space. Another thing he later had misgivings about was the liberal quantity of new windows punched in what was an almost blind exterior wall, thus detracting from the original spirit of the castle. His explanation was that, coming from London, the Conways were used to more light than was traditionally found in a medieval castle.

Imaginatively Caroe tried to persuade Conway to move Crosby Hall, the surviving great hall of a fifteenth-century house built for a wealthy wool merchant, to Allington following the demolition of Crosby Place in the City in 1908, but Conway resisted this temptation.

Conway regularly contributed articles on architectural subjects such as 'Kentish Cottages' to *Country Life* and knew its proprietor, Edward Hudson, well. He recorded in his diary: 'Hudson arrived [at Allington] in the rain and we went out at once under umbrellas and all round the outside of the castle and he was full of praise and wonder at our pluck.'[96]

By the outbreak of the First World War about half the castle had been restored. In a series of articles about Allington in *Country Life* in May 1918, Conway seemed far from certain that he would complete the restoration.

By then Conway had fallen out with Caroe, 'who had a pugnacious disposition', and replaced him with Philip Tilden, whom he had met through his daughter in 1917, and 'engaged [him] at £2 a week'.[97] It was a bleak time for Tilden, as no one was commissioning new work, and this proved to be a pivotal point in his career: over the next decade or so Conway would be responsible for nearly all of his important commissions.

With a war on at first Tilden could do no more than plan and lay out an extensive new Italianate garden, which featured 1,000 feet/305 metres of yew hedges enclosing geometrical parterres each filled with flowers of a single kind, for example lilies. But as the war came to an end he was able to continue the process of restoration and rebuilding, beginning with the construction of a new gatehouse at the entrance to the drive:

a double cottage with an arch between, completed in 1920. The Conways used this for fleeting winter visits. When they were resident in the castle during the summer, the gatehouse could be let furnished to tenants. Tilden was to work at Allington intermittently until 1933, restoring both Solomon's Tower and the great hall.

An unexpected and charmingly quirky detail at Allington is the decoration of the windowsill in the entrance hall of the castle with fragments of antique Persian tiles; several other windows have plaster casts by D. Brucciania and Co.[98]

Allington made a splendid setting for Conway's collections. 'We intended Allington Castle to be made a kind of casket to contain such works of art as we had acquired, or might in future acquire,' he wrote.[99] Indeed he regarded the castle as another addition to his collections: 'A castle is merely another kind of work of art, as delightful to collect, to study, to repair, to live with as is a fine picture. If I were rich I should be greatly tempted to collect several castles . . . I know of a

LEFT Allington Castle
from the north.

dozen [castles] or more that could be repaired and made into glorious modern homes.'[100] But he was most disappointed that it proved unsuitable for displaying his fine collection of paintings, which included a Giorgione, as the positioning of the windows resulted in very poor light.

Conway's diaries make frequent references to jaunts to look at other castles: for example on 22 May 1912 he notes 'Goodrich Castle, full of interest . . . might be perfectly repaired and would be a lovely home' and the following day he dismisses St Donat's as 'not a patch on what Allington would be'.[101]

On Conway's death in 1931, their only child, Agnes, inherited the castle and let it to Alfred Bossom, MP for Maidstone.[102] In 1946 Agnes and her husband, George Horsfield, an eminent archaeologist, returned to live at Allington. She died in 1950. The following year, Knight Frank sold the contents and George Horsfield sold Allington to the Carmelite Friars from Aylesford for £15,000.

In 1996 Sir Robert and Lady Worcester bought Allington and over the years they have been able to buy back several of the Conways' furnishings. Sir Robert was born in Kansas City and as a leading Anglo-American (he was for many years chairman of the Anglo-American society the Pilgrims) he is an apt inheritor and custodian of a castle that owes its survival and restoration to the single-minded determination of an English polymath and the money of his American stepfather-in-law.

NOTES

ALLINGTON CASTLE

83 Joan Evans, *The Conways: A History of Three Generations*, Museum Press, 1966, p. 204

84 Ibid.

85 Sir Martin Conway, *The Sport of Collecting,* Frederick A. Stokes, New York, 1914, p. 134

86 Joan Evans, *The Conways: A History of Three Generations*, Museum Press, 1966, p. 205

87 Aymer Vallance (b.1862) was a scion of a wealthy brewing family from Sittingbourne, Kent. In 1920 he bought Stoneacre, near Maidstone, Kent, a Wealden hall house, and restored it. It is now a property of the National Trust (see note 102).

88 In 1720 Allington was bought by Sir Robert Marsham, 1st Lord Romney, a remote descendant of the Wyatts. He was created an earl by George III. At the end of the nineteenth century, the 5th Earl (of the second creation) was forced by local outcry not to demolish the castle.

89 Conway of Allington, Martin Conway, Ist Baron, Cambridge University Library

90 Sir Martin Conway, 'Allington Castle', *Country Life*, 4 May 1918, p. 427

91 Molly Berkeley, *Beaded Bubbles*, Hamish Hamilton, 1967, p. 72

92 Kenneth Clark, *The Other Half: A Self-Portrait,* John Murray, 1977

93 Joan Evans, *The Conways: A History of Three Generations*, Museum Press, 1966, p. 205

94 Katrina Conway, 29 September 1905, the Conway Papers, University of Cambridge Library

95 Sir Martin Conway, 'Allington Castle', *Country Life*, 4 May 1918

96 Conway, Diary, 8 February 1912, the Conway Papers, University of Cambridge Library

97 Conway, Diary, 30 May 1917, the Conway Papers, University of Cambridge Library

98 'From the middle of the nineteenth-century casts of many objects from both the British Museum and the Victoria & Albert Museum were supplied under license by the firm of Brucciani & Co. This firm was taken over by the Victoria & Albert Museum in 1922': David Wilson, *The History of the British Musuem*, British Museum Press, 2002, p. 359

99 Sir Martin Conway, *The Sport of Collecting,* Frederick A. Stokes, New York, 1914, p. 146

100 Sir Martin Conway, 'Allington Castle', *Country Life*, 4 May 1918, p. 427

101 Conway, Diary, 22 May 1912, the Conway Papers, University of Cambridge Library

102 Alfred Charles Bossom, later 1st Baron Bossom (1881–1965), an architect and politician, author of *Building to the Skies: The Romance of the Skyscraper*, The Studio, 1934. He owned Stoneacre, near Maidstone, Kent, a medieval hall house which had earlier belonged to Aymer Vallance (see note 87).

CASTLE DROGO
DEVON

'The ultimate justification of Drogo is that it does not pretend to be a castle. It is a castle, as a castle is built, of granite, on a mountain, in the twentieth century,' writes Christopher Hussey.[103]

Julius Drewe, Drogo's creator, was – along with Thomas Lipton and John James Sainsbury – among a growing band of mercantile adventurers who made vast fortunes providing household provisions for the ever-expanding middle classes of the late nineteenth and early twentieth centuries, and he embodied all the social aspirations of an Edwardian self-made millionaire. For him a house, however large, would simply not do – a castle it had to be.

Born in 1856, Drew (he added the 'e' later) was the son of the Reverend George Smith Drew and his wife, Mary, née Peek. Both came from respectable grocery families – Meredith & Drew and Peek, Frean & Company. The young

LEFT Julius Drewe, painted by George Harcourt in 1931.

RIGHT The view over Dartmoor from the roof terrace. The main stairs window is discernible in the east front.

Julius began his working life as tea buyer in China. On returning to England at the age of twenty-two, he opened his first shop, The Willow Pattern Tea Store, in Liverpool in 1878, selling cut-price tea straight from China to the public. In 1883 he and his partner, John Musker, set up the Home and Colonial Stores in the Edgware Road in London. By 1890 they had 107 shops all over the country. As the majority shareholder receiving large dividends, Drew was an exceedingly wealthy man and at the age of thirty-three he retired from an active role in the business. He then transferred his energy and drive into establishing himself as a country gentleman.

In 1890 Drew had married Frances Richardson, the daughter of a cotton manufacturer. They set up home in Culverden Castle, an early nineteenth-century battlemented house near Tunbridge Wells in Kent. Nine years later Drew bought Wadhurst Hall, a huge red-brick mansion that had been built in 1877 for two Spanish bachelor brothers, Adrian and Cristobal de Murrietta, who had had extensive interests in South America and had gone bankrupt because of the Argentine default on bond payments.

It must have been exhilarating for the arriviste Drew to see himself listed for the first time in *Burke's Landed Gentry* in 1906 as 'Drew of Wadhurst Hall'. He had been granted arms and a crest in 1899, based on the medieval arms of Drew (Ermine a lion passant Gules).[104] He lived the life of a typical squire, sending his sons to Eton, shooting, fishing, visiting Scotland and undertaking philanthropic works in the neighbourhood. But, *Burke's* notwithstanding, like so many other nouveaux riches he was anxious to further consolidate his newfound social status.

Julius's elder barrister brother, William, was interested in genealogy and discovered through a genealogist that the Drews could lay claim to hailing originally from Devon, being descended from one Norman Drogo de Teigne, who had given his name to the parish of Drewsteignton on the edge of Exmoor. By happy coincidence, Mrs Drew's cousin had been the rector there. Acting with alacrity, Drewe added an 'e' to his name apparently in an attempt to make it look more distinguished and bought 450 acres/182 hectares to the south and west of Drewsteignton. Fortuitously the previous year he had sold his remaining shares in H&C for £1 million, a staggering sum for the time.

According to Basil Drewe, Julius's youngest son, it was Edward Hudson, the owner of *Country Life*, who recommended Edwin Lutyens to his father as 'the only possible architect' to build a new castle on the Devon acres. At the time Lutyens

ABOVE Left: Julius Drewe, Sir Edwin Lutyens and John Walker in 1910. Centre: The north tower and the bathroom wing. Right: Seen from afar, Castle Drogo has a medieval air.

was busy restoring Lindisfarne Castle for Hudson (see page 62).

'I do wish he didn't want a castle but just a delicious lovable house with plenty of good large rooms in it,' wrote Edwin Lutyens to his wife on 3 August 1910. At this stage in his career Lutyens had yet to design a country house let alone a castle and understandably he was apprehensive about the commission. 'Mr. Drewe writes a nice and exciting letter to go on with the drawings not more than £50,000 though and £10,000 for the garden,' wrote Lutyens.[105] But Drewe's ambitious dreams knew no bounds, and just a week later Lutyens was again writing to his wife: 'He wants to build a large keep or Commemorative Tower, to commemorate the first Drogo, and this will be over and beyond the £60,000.'[106] Four years before the outbreak of the First World War, Drewe was oblivious to the portentous rumblings of the social upheaval that would come in its wake. He clearly believed he was commissioning an ancestral seat to support a dynasty that would stretch far beyond the new century into the centuries to come.

After much deliberation (in a letter to his wife Lutyens recounts a picnic with the Drewe family while deciding where to build) a suitable site for the castle was chosen, on a granite outcrop 900 feet/274 metres above sea level overlooking a steep gorge, commanding a breathtaking view over the River Teign and the surrounding wild terrain of Dartmoor.

Lutyens began working up the first rough sketches on a voyage to South Africa in November 1910 and finalized the first scheme in the following April. The first plans were for a castle arranged around a courtyard, with the entrance to the north and a vast great hall with gothic windows between buttresses on the south, on the edge of the crag overlooking the River Teign. By 1911 this had evolved into a more compact plan with an open court facing north.

In November Lutyens 'made the crucial decision to splay the sides of the courtyard outwards by moving the domestic and service wings through 20 degrees – it is this angle which adds to the picturesque drama of the spectacular fragment of Drogo that was built,' according to Gavin Stamp. One problem was that the brief was confusingly vague. 'The lack of certainty at Drogo meant that only visual requirements were left to predominate and the house could only depend on ideas about massing and movement through a sequence of spaces.'[107]

LEFT The portcullis and heraldic Drewe lion on the entrance tower. An arrow slit in the shape of an inverted cross.

RIGHT The five-sided chapel protrudes from the south front of Castle Drogo.

FOLLOWING PAGES Left: The head of the monumental central staircase, with vaulted granite ceilings and arches. Right: Looking up the theatrical stairs ascending from the dining room.

Drewe's insistence on 6-foot/1.75-metre-thick walls (Lutyens had originally planned a 2-foot/60-centimetre cavity between two 2-foot-thick walls) meant that the overall cost rapidly escalated and as a result the plans were drastically scaled down to just the eastern half of the castle. Lutyens was unhappy with this and tried to persuade Drewe to extend the northern wing with a screen and a castellated gateway over the approach drive – even going so far as to have a full-size timber and tarpaulin mock-up built and erected in the stifling hot summer of 1913. Drewe was not to be persuaded.

The foundation stone was laid on Julius Drewe's fifty-fifth birthday on 4 April 1911. More than a hundred men were employed on site, working a fifty-hour week with half an hour off for lunch. A further forty men worked in the site granite quarry nearby, also on Dartmoor. Any untoward behaviour and the miscreant was given half an hour's notice. But the outbreak of the First World War hampered progress. More than three-quarters of the builders enlisted, and by January 1917 work had stopped altogether.

The death of the Drewes' adored eldest son, Adrian (named after Adrian de Murrieta), at the Battle of Ypres in 1917 was a shattering blow to his parents. Adrian had been as enthusiastic about Castle Drogo as his father. 'The joy very much went out of life as far as my father and mother were concerned . . . my

father really was something of an invalid afterwards,' recalled Frances, his youngest sister.[108] But Drewe's two younger sons cajoled him into finishing Drogo. And after the war George Dillistone designed the terraced formal gardens.

The last stone was laid on 22 December 1925 and the Drewes finally moved in properly in 1927, but the castle was not finished until 1930, sadly only a year before the deaths of Julius Drewe and John Walker, the clerk of works and master mason, who had overseen the work almost from the beginning.

From afar Drogo resembles a solid medieval fortress rising up on its granite outcrop amidst a wild untamed landscape. Its pronounced robust character is achieved by Lutyens's stark uncompromising design, subtly composed of massive walls punctuated by a play of levels and bends. It is, as Gavin Stamp observes, an 'astonishing essay in the sculptural handling of planes of granite – inside as well as out'.[109]

The imposing entrance tower, complete with a massive 644lb/292kg working portcullis, breaks forward from the west front. It is skilfully articulated in a delightfully understated manner by the use of a slightly projecting granite course about 9 feet/2.75 metres from the ground, creating an overhang of about 2 inches/5 centimetres, which breaks up the façade of the tower and emphasizes

the slenderness of the corner turrets. A quirky detail in such an uncompromising building is the arrow slits in the shape of an inverted cross in the two turrets.

The use of the local granite accentuates the monumentality of the whole, particularly on the east front, where the structure rises up sheer from the ground, as if it is growing out of the very bowels of the moor. 'It is unlikely that there is any house in this country where the material of the structure has such a dominating effect as that produced by the granite of Castle Drogo. It is built throughout of this harsh, glittering rather porous stone,' reported *Country Life*.[110] Drewe instructed Lutyens to keep the ashlar façades as plain as possible in the interests of historical authenticity. The lack of dripstones on the mullioned and transomed windows, combined with the lack of waterspouts, also in the spirit of historic accuracy, on such an exposed site proved to be foolish in the extreme, making the entire façade permanently susceptible to rain.

Bravely embracing new building materials, Lutyens used concrete and steel for the floors and the flat roof; and he used asphalt, then a new material brought from pits in the Caribbean, to prevent water penetration by inserting a vertical layer between the internal and external faces of the 24–36-inch/60–90-centimetre-thick solid blocks. This vertical asphalt skin was continued through to roof level, where it joined a horizontal asphalt screed. The use of asphalt was disastrous: the roof had begun to leak even before the building was finished. 'Lutyens did not really understand how asphalt works. He thought of it as a panacea, curing all ills. Of course it gets restrained and then cracks. It was leaking from day one,' says Mehmet Berker of Inskip & Jenkins, project architect for a recent programme of repairs.[111]

Nevertheless what is immediately striking about the castle is the meticulous care Lutyens took over every single detail, whether in the main reception rooms or the service quarters. The manipulation of space is majestic in its bravado, as seen particularly on the great main staircase. The descent of the three flights from the drawing room to the dining room is a *coup de théâtre*, around an angle of 90 degrees. Above the staircase, the ceiling is manipulated with superb aplomb by Lutyens, beginning as a coffered granite vault until the turn, where another shallow dome eases the change of direction. A further vault between two arches follows, finally turning into

OPPOSITE The kitchen was probably inspired by the banking halls of the Bank of England, designed by Sir John Soane.

LEFT The scullery, with a table designed by Sir Edwin Lutyens.

FOLLOWING PAGES
Left, clockwise from top left: The entrance hall, looking towards the library door; a bath from Messrs Boulding, London, chosen personally by Julius Drewe; the interior of the chapel, consecrated in September 1931, two months before Drewe's death; levers and dials in the Switch Room. Right, clockwise from top left: The entrance hall, looking towards the drawing room; the billiard table was designed by Lutyens and made by Burroughs & Watts; the butler's pantry with the bell board; the drawing room is lit by windows on three sides.

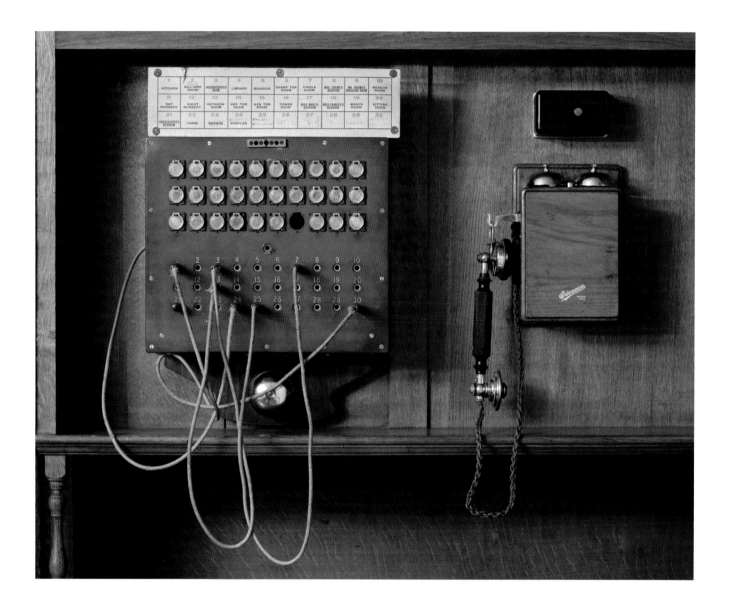

an oak-beamed ceiling, but still at the same height as the dome. The staircase is lit by a east-facing mullioned window of monumental proportions, with forty-eight leaded lights and transoms subtly graded in size to augment the effect of perspective, creating the illusion of dizzying height. The top-lit domed kitchen, scullery and larder were almost certainly inspired by Sir John Soane's banking halls at the Bank of England, which were torn down in the 1920s.

In the main reception rooms the Drewes installed the de Muriettas' collection of inlaid Spanish furniture and large tapestries originally at Wadhurst Hall, a welcome exotic flourish against the severe backdrop of the granite walls. The unrelenting granite construction is always in evidence throughout the castle, even when progressively softened by overlays of oak, painted panelling and plaster.

Behind the trappings of a castle apparently steeped in history was an early twentieth-century country house that

boasted the latest in modern technology. There was an integral centralized vacuuming system in all the main rooms: the maid could plug a brush, pole and flexible tube into a discreet socket in the wall and dust from the floor would be vacuumed into a receptacle in the basement. Electricity for the castle was generated by a turbine house designed by Lutyens and situated 200 feet/61 metres below the castle on the opposite bank of the Teign. There were more than three hundred electrical plug sockets; and as early as 1915 a telephone exchange was installed, connecting to eighteen telephones placed throughout the castle as well as in two servants' cottages.

The best known of all British twentieth-century castles, Drogo is a compellingly sophisticated monument to both the grandiose dreams of the grocer Drewe and to the architectural brilliance and imagination of Sir Edwin Lutyens. However, Julius's dynastic dream did not last long. Less than fifty years

after his death, his grandson, Anthony, gave Castle Drogo to the National Trust in 1974. On visiting Drogo shortly after the Trust took possession, James Lees-Milne observed with characteristic sharpness: 'a new family aspiring to, rather arriving at, landed gentryhood, and now the representative living upstairs in a tiny flat, all within my lifetime'.[112]

OPPOSITE The telephone exchange, installed in 1915. The butler could direct an incoming call to any one of eighteen telephones in the castle and to two servants' cottages.

ABOVE A view of the battlemented roof terrace.

NOTES

CASTLE DROGO

103 Christopher Hussey, *The Life of Sir Edwin Lutyens*, Country Life, 1953, p. 225

104 David White, *Somerset Herald*, in an email to Amicia de Moubray, 5 June 2010

105 Sir Edwin Lutyens to Lady Emily Lutyens, 3 August 1910

106 Ibid., 9 September 1910

107 Gavin Stamp, *Sir Edwin Lutyens: Country Houses from the Archives of Country Life,* Aurum Press, 2001

108 *Castle Drogo* (guidebook), National Trust, 1995, p. 46

109 Gavin Stamp, *Sir Edwin Lutyens: Country Houses from the Archives of Country Life*, Aurum Press, 2001

110 A.S.G. Butler, 'Castle Drogo, Devonshire', *Country Life*, 10 August 1945

111 Isabel Allen, 'The Building is in a State of Semi-Undress but It Bears the Indignity Rather Well', A Building Study, *The Architects' Journal*, 21 June 2007, p. 26

112 James Lees-Milne, Diary, 9 September 1976, *Through Wood and Dale: Diaries 1975–1978*, John Murray, 1998

HERSTMONCEUX CASTLE
EAST SUSSEX

'To come suddenly as one does, over the rim of the oak and bracken clad saucer in which Herstmonceux lies, and see these rose and gold and silver and purple patinated towers rising out of what is in effect a great glassy lake, is to see the Fairy Castle of all romances made manifest, yet a fairy land that is the very essence of England.'[113]

Country Life was describing the restored Herstmonceux Castle, a stately ruby-red castle near Hailsham in East Sussex that is one of the oldest brick buildings in England, dating in part from the late fifteenth century. Brick became fashionable in the fifteenth century when it was used to build royal palaces such as Sheen in Surrey and the Manor of the More in Hertfordshire. In 1441 Sir Roger de Fiennes, Treasurer of the Household of Henry VI, was granted the King's licence to crenellate and replaced the existing manor house at Herstmonceaux with a castle.

Approached from the east, the square castle sits in a deep hollow surrounded by an ancient park. Each façade measures just over 200 feet/61 metres, and at the corners rise four great octagonal towers. The whole structure is dominated by the magnificent gatehouse in the south façade. This, the main façade, has a pleasing rhythm of elements: from one side to the other there is a tower, a turret, the gatehouse, a turret and a tower. Each of the other three sides has a semi-octagonal tower.

The inspiration for the main courtyard at Herstmonceux came from Eton College, founded by Henry VI in 1440 and dedicated to the Virgin. John Rowelond is recorded as present at Herstmonceux in 1436 and his name is also mentioned in the Eton building accounts.

In 1708 Thomas, Lord Dacre sold Herstmonceux to George Naylor of Lincoln's Inn. His heir was his nephew Francis Hare, the Bishop of Chichester and tutor to Robert Walpole while he was at Cambridge. Hare's eldest son, Francis, died after 'a life of the wildest dissipation (he was a member of the Hellfire Club) without leaving any children by his wife, who was his stepmother's sister'.[114] Herstmonceux was inherited by his half-brother, Robert, whose first wife, Sarah, died 'very suddenly after eating ices when overheated at a ball'.[115] Soon afterwards Robert married the wealthy Henrietta Henckel, 'a woman designing and bad'.[116]

In 1777 the new Mrs Hare instructed the architect Samuel Wyatt to survey the castle and, probably hoping to be commissioned to build a replacement,

LEFT Herstmonceux Castle, before restoration.

LEFT A cartoon by Sir
Max Beerbohm of Claude
Lowther MP.

to Herstmonceux in childish senility and 'wander round and round the castle ruins in the early morning and late evening, wringing her hands and saying – "Who could have done such a wicked thing, as to pull down this old place?" Then her daughters, Caroline and Marianne, walking beside her, would say – "Oh dear mamma, it was you who did it, you know" – and she would despairingly resume – "Oh no, that is impossible."'[118]

In the nineteenth century the castle changed hands several times and became progressively more and more forlorn but increasingly romantic, smothered in swathes of ivy. It was a popular place to visit, particularly towards the end of the century, when a tea garden operated inside the ruins with tables in the courtyard behind the remains of the South Gatehouse. Admission to the estate was sixpence, and picnic parties were allowed outside the castle walls. Vita Sackville-West captures the spirit of the place then: 'Lost among the oaks and bracken of Sussex, the sea not far away, there was a beauty of desolation, a nobility in ruin which supplied a fantasy that restoration, however skilful, can never recapture.'[119]

It was awakened from its reverie by the wealthy Colonel Claude Lowther, who bought it in 1911. After a distinguished war record in South Africa, Lowther had been elected MP for Eskdale in 1910. He was the son of Francis William Lowther, an illegitimate son of the 2nd Earl of Lowther and Louise Beatrice de Fonblanque, an opera singer. Colonel Lowther was a singular character. According to his obituary in *The Times* (18 June 1929) he was 'known as one of a group of brilliant young Conservative members . . . He seemed destined for a notable career.' He was also a great aesthete and a connoisseur. 'He possessed an inspired flair for recognizing and acquiring beautiful objects of all kinds.'[120] He wrote various books and plays, and he was something of a dandy. 'His dress often recalled a more picturesque age,' said *The Times*. 'His check suits were sometimes in so pronounced a pattern that Maud [wife of Sir Herbert] Beerbohm Tree once called him "Colonel Loud Clother."'[121]

he recommended its demolition as dangerous and unsafe. The following year the contents were sold over the course of three days, with prospective buyers camping out in front of the castle. Shortly afterwards demolition began. 'This gothic barbarity was perpetrated and the stately and princely abode of the Fiennes and Dacres was demolished for the purpose of erecting with the materials a modern dwelling,' lamented the Revd E.E. Crake.[117] Only the great south gatehouse and the outer walls remained.

Mrs Hare lived to a great age and when 'the burden of her years came on her' she repented of her avarice and injustice, and, according to Augustus Hare, would come back

RIGHT The gatehouse
before restoration.

At the time of Lowther's purchase 'the process of decay was proceeding apace; portions of the great wall fell every year. The moat was silted up and ivy was threatening to engulf much of the castle. The days of the ruin were numbered,' according to *Country Life*.[122] Possibly Lowther's purchase of Herstmonceux was inspired by the vast Lowther Castle in Cumbria, built by the young Robert Smirke in 1811 for his grandfather, the 2nd Earl of Lonsdale of the second creation. It must have been galling to know that as an illegitimate descendant he had no claim on this magnificent castle.

Lowther did not attempt a perfect, authentic restoration. Conway writes in *Episodes in a Varied Life* that Lowther 'frankly cared nothing about archaeology or historical correctness. His lovely ruins were to be shaped by addition or removals into the most beautiful whole that he could devise.'[123] He demonstrated supreme Edwardian self-confidence in demolishing the remains of the domestic buildings within the walls, and he drastically changed the configuration of the original layout, dispensing with the four internal courtyards and replacing them with just one.

'In place of a complex medieval plan an attractive and not particularly distinguished house in a loosely late gothic style was created around a single courtyard. To accommodate this design, almost all that remained of the original plan was swept away, an operation justified on grounds of cost,'[124] writes John Goodall.

He chose to concentrate on the south façade, which includes the majestic gatehouse tower section. Much of the work is believed to have been executed to his own plan, though he did enlist a little known architect, Cecil Perkins. They sensitively reused many of the original bricks salvaged from the ruins (machicolations and the tops of some of the turrets), employing builders who had been trained to work in the manner of the original craftsmen so that it was almost impossible to discern the new 'repairs'. Lowther bought a wall in Hastings, thought to have been originally part of Hastings Castle, to be used in the restoration of the banqueting hall. Lowther restored the west side up to the outer wall of the new Drummers Hall and on the east side, the work was completed as far as the outer walls of the chapel. The remainder was to be deliberately left as a ruin and incorporated into the garden. The shell of the Drummers Hall was finished when the First World War broke out, the tracery design for its windows inspired by an antique piece of French woodwork owned by Lowther. He filled the restored rooms with his extensive collections of fine tapestries and antique furniture. Like many collectors of the era he was also partial to architectural salvage. A notable addition was a staircase said to have come from Theobalds Palace, a house in Hertfordshire once owned by Sir William Cecil. Lord Conway

Herstmonceux Castle.

wrote, 'Colonel Lowther possesses an almost unique power of creating in every room he decorated an air of romance,' while in 1929 *Country Life* opined: 'All he has done is felicitous in contriving a picturesque habitation in which modern tastes temper archaeological exactitude.'[125]

The castle made a great impression on all who visited it. 'I shall never forget our first glimpse of this enchanted castle – a castle in a dream which must surely dissolve and vanish at our approach,'[126] wrote Violet Bonham Carter, who also evocatively describes the eccentric atmosphere Lowther cultivated at Herstmonceux:

> We were greeted by Claude Lowther dressed in black knee-breeches, black silk stockings and buckled shoes as though for a Court Ball. 'But – is there a party?' I stammered breathlessly (not liking to ask point-blank whether the King was expected). 'No – we are alone – except for Mrs. Cornwallis-West, who hasn't arrived . . .'
>
> When I came down to dinner I was startled by the sight of a vast ram with muddy hooves and clotted pelt roaming at large among the priceless furniture and objets d'art. It broke into a sudden canter and nearly knocked down Mrs. West who screamed: 'What is this animal doing here?' Our host replied: 'This animal, as you call him, is my beloved Peter – the mascot of my Territorial Battalion, "Lowther's Lambs".[127] He has the freedom of the Castle and comes and goes when and where he chooses.'[128]

Like Astor at Hever (see page 48), Lowther was passionately interested in the occult. But the notoriety of Herstmonceux's ghostly tales made it a difficult property to sell after Lowther's early death at the age of fifty-three. (The contents were dispersed in a two-day sale by Christie's.) When it was put up to auction bidders refused to go above $175,000, although the estimate was nearer $1 million. Eventually the 35-year-old Reginald Lawson, grandson of Lionel Lawson, one of the founders of the *Daily Telegraph*, and his American wife purchased it. 'Romantic Mystery of the Famous Castle Nobody Wanted to Buy Until . . . Along Came a Brave American Girl Who Scoffs at Ghosts and Just Adores Haunted Rooms' proclaimed a headline in *The Ogden Standard Examiner* in January 1930.

OPPOSITE Above: the drawing room; below: the ante-room to the drawing room.
LEFT The east corridor and flight of stairs opposite the chapel.

LEFT The Elizabethan
staircase, reputedly
from Theobalds Palace,
Hertfordshire.

RIGHT The new
banqueting hall.

castle. Lowther had already extended the southern arm to approximately double its original width. It was presumably a complete square in the fifteenth century.

Four years after the restoration was completed the Second World War broke out. In 1941 Latham was arrested for alleged offences against military law; it was the first occasion since 1815 that an MP serving in the army had been arrested and tried by court martial.[129] He was found guilty and sent to prison for two years. Not surprisingly, at the end of the war he sold the castle; it was bought by the Admiralty and it became the home of the Royal Observatory, Greenwich. It has been owned since 1989 by the International Study Centre of Queen's University (Canada).

Less than twelve months later, in December 1930, Reginald was found shot in the woods at Saltwood Castle, which the Lawsons also owned (see page 144), and after his death his widow shut herself away in Saltwood and put Herstmonceux up for sale.

Two years after Lawson's death, it was purchased by Sir Paul Latham Bt (1905–55), who was also an MP (for Scarborough). Latham, whose wealth came from the silk trade, completed the restoration of the castle, with the help of the architect Walter Godfrey. A noted antiquary and topographical historian, Godfrey was the first director of and the inspiration behind the National Buildings Record (the basis of the National Monuments Record) and contributed regularly to the *Architectural Review*. Later in his career he was to design an Arts and Crafts house incorporating the ruins of Leybourne Castle in Kent. Latham's approach was much more purist and scholarly than that of Lowther, who yearned for a softer, altogether dreamier effect, and he returned to the original design of high-pitched roofs rising about the crenellations. He finished the chapel and banqueting hall and reconstructed the north side of the castle, installing libraries on the ground floor and a ballroom on the first floor. Photographs of the interiors in Latham's time reveal a highly sophisticated eye. The Ladies Bower, for example, is sparsely furnished with fine eighteenth-century English and European antiques judiciously arranged with a fine array of Persian carpets, giving it the appearance of a grand reception room in a Venetian palazzo.

In 1933 Latham widened, cleared and reflooded the moat, which lies around the south and eastern sides of the

NOTES

HERSTMONCEAUX CASTLE

113 *Country Life*, 30 November 1935
114 Augustus J.C. Hare, *The Story of My Life: Volume 1*, George Allen, 1896, p. 2
115 Ibid., p. 3
116 Ian C. Hannah, *The Sussex Coast,* T. Fisher Unwin, 1912, p. 317
117 Reverend E.E. Crake, *The Castle and the Church of Hurstmonceux*, Farncombe & Co., 1897, p. 24
118 Augustus J.C. Hare, *The Story of My Life: Volume 1*, George Allen, 1896, pp. 3–4
119 V. Sackville-West, *The English Country House,* William Collins, 1945, p.15
120 Violet Bonham Carter, *Winston Churchill as I Knew Him,* Eyre & Spottiswoode and Collins, 1965
121 Hesketh Pearson, *Beerbohm Tree: His Life and Laughter,* Methuen & Co., 1956, p. 145
122 *Country Life*, 1918
123 Sir Martin Conway, *Episodes in a Varied Life,* Country Life, 1932
124 John Goodall, article in *The Burlington Magazine*, August 2004
125 'Herstmonceux Castle', *Country Life*, 18 May 1929, p. 708
126 Violet Bonham Carter, *Winston Churchill as I Knew Him*, Eyre & Spottiswoode & Collins, 1965, p. 463
127 In September 1914 Lowther raised and equipped the 11th, 12th and 13th Battalions of the Royal Sussex Regiment, who became known as 'Lowther's Lambs'. His regiment was highly successful, enlisting men from the South Downs already bound to one another by community ties.
128 Violet Bonham Carter, *Winston Churchill as I Knew Him*, Eyre & Spottiswoode & Collins, 1965, p. 464
129 *The Times*, 26 July 1955

DUNDERAVE

ARGYLL

'"Beetling against the breakers, very cold, very arrogant upon its barren promontory" stands the Tower of Dunderave. The older part was rehabilitated with all the sympathy, understanding and delight in craftsmanship that is associated with Lorimer's work. The lyrical effect of this castle rising from its setting by the loch-side, its minute scale, the exquisite feel of its rooms, as they flow one into another, and the tender delicacy of their detail, together makes this dwelling a place of enchantment,'[130] writes the architect Oliver Hill.

Dunderave is a superlative example of an intensely romantic restoration of a typical Scottish tower house. It was commissioned in 1911 from Sir Robert Lorimer by Sir Andrew Noble for his daughter, Lily.

A wealthy Scottish Edwardian tycoon, Noble had made his fortune in the Tyneside shipbuilding and armaments firm Armstrong Whitworth, and like so many other arrivistes scanned the pages of *Country Life* in search of a bucolic retreat. In 1905 he spotted the Ardkinglas estate on Loch Fyne in Argyll, and snapping it up commissioned Lorimer to build him a substantial mansion worthy of his newfound wealth. The last house on the site had been burnt in 1831.

LEFT Dunderave from the north-west before restoration.

RIGHT Sir Robert Lorimer (1864–1929), painted in 1886 by John Henry Lorimer.

FOLLOWING PAGES Dunderave sits on a small promontory at the northern end of Loch Fyne.

The ruined tower of Dunderave – it would be immortalized as 'The Castle of Doom' in Neil Munro's romantic novel of that name, published in 1911 – stood directly opposite the Nobles' new house on the other side of the loch, in the manner of an eighteenth-century eye-catcher. The tower was soon the family's favourite picnicking spot.

According to an inscription over the door Dunderave was built by the chieftain of the MacNachtans, a clan recorded in Argyll since the thirteenth century. They consolidated their position by judicious alignment with the powerful Campbells of Argyll and were rewarded with lands on Loch Fyne in 1473. At the beginning of the eighteenth century the lands passed to the Campbells of Ardkinglas. It was abandoned early in the nineteenth century. In the eighteenth century Dunderave went by marriage with Ardkinglas to the Livingstone family and was last inhabited at the beginning of the nineteenth century.

Dunderave is a tall traditional L-plan tower house with a pleasingly picturesque profile. At the time of building a certain degree of self-defensiveness was necessary in an area still riven by feuding factions. But as in Dunderave's southern counterparts its external appearance masks the reality that within the thick walls is the residence of a civilized Scottish laird. 'Dunderave's asymmetrical profile . . . is deceptively

sophisticated, coinciding with the flowering of this romantic Scottish building type,' wrote *Country Life*.[131]

The major hurdle Lorimer had to overcome was how to provide the requisite Edwardian servant accommodation (old Highland lairds lived in far simpler conditions, banishing their serfs to the basements) and commensurate domestic offices, as well as the additional sitting rooms required, without detracting from the silhouette of the original tower house.

Lorimer's inspired solution was to add two wings, one pierced by a dramatic vaulted passage through to a secluded inner courtyard. Before any building work began, Lorimer erected full-sized wooden skeletons of the proposed additions to ensure that they did not compromise the tower. He then altered the position of the wings, making the whole ensemble less rigid, so that they are at a slightly irregular, splayed angle, thus greatly enhancing the romantic composition of the whole by allowing the tower to soar over the wings, 'accentuating the grim mass'.[132] It looks as if, like Topsy, the castle 'just growed', acquiring accretions in a delightfully haphazard manner over time.

In essence Lorimer's sensitive restoration does not alter the overall conception of the existing structure. Indeed, from the loch its stirring silhouette remains unchanged. His only

LEFT Dunderave, painted by
John Young Hunter in 1906.

RIGHT The sixteenth-century
tower with additions designed by
Sir Robert Lorimer on the right.

structural change was to break through openings into the new wings. He sensibly added the new kitchen to the back of the old one, thus enabling the flues to be carried up the original chimney. Fortunately, it was a huge shaft and he was able to hide all the sanitary pipes, bath wastes and heating pipes within it.

Logistically, Dunderave must have been a difficult project to manage, for it is buried deep in the Highlands. Before any work could commence on constructing Ardkinglas House a pier had had to be built into the loch – everything bar the actual stone for the walls had to be imported.

The loggia at Dunderave connecting the tower to the new principal sitting room echoes the one on the north front of Ardkinglas. It is a surprisingly Italianate feature to find in the Highlands but, as Christopher Hussey writes, 'it [the loggia]

is particularly desirable in our fresh-air loving age, the more so at Dunderave, which commands enchanting views up and down the loch.' Somewhat eccentrically in such a weather-torn region (a south-westerly gale can blow very smartly up the loch), the only route to the library is via the loggia. Lorimer gave the Nobles the opportunity to reject this oddity, but they decided that 'the charms were estimated to exceed the drawbacks'. To those who were up to braving the elements the reward was an intimate secluded library, with a barrel-vaulted hand-modelled seventeenth-century-style plaster ceiling giving it the air of a 'cosy casket'. As Hussey eloquently writes, 'On a blustering night when the waves lash the sea-wall below, its diminutive size gives rise to a warming of the heart's cockles, a sensation aptly called that of being snug.'[133]

The interior is finished with Lorimer's characteristic attention to understated detail, which is subtly enlivened by the surprising but imaginative choice of raw bird's-eye maple wainscoting in the bedrooms, simple wrought-iron balustrades executed by Thomas Hadden and enchanting plaster ceilings hand-modelled in the seventeenth-century style by Lorimer's protégés Sam Wilson and Thomas Beattie.

Lorimer disastrously tore off what remained of the original protective harling, leaving the tower and the north-west front susceptible to penetration by the wind-driven rains that hurl up Loch Fyne. Dark stains are discernible on the masonry in *Country Life* photographs of 1931. (The Edwardians thought little of harling and Lorimer also ripped off what remained at his earlier restoration of another tower house, Earlshall in

Fife.) As a result severe water penetration has been a long-running problem at Dunderave ever since.

In 1947 Dunderave was sold, appropriately to another industrialist, the 1st Viscount Weir (1877–1959), who bought it for his son, John. His wife, Marguerite, outlived him, battling with the damp until her death in 1987. The next owner, Barry Weir (no relation), was unable to solve the problem.

The current owner, Dr Stephen Joffe, a South African pioneer of laser/keyhole surgery, has glazed the loggia, turning it into a sitting room, which, though understandable in a less hardy era, means that the tangible link with the sublime surroundings that must have dramatically enhanced the experience of staying or living at Dunderave has been lost. However, he is to be congratulated for solving the water

OPPOSITE The library designed by Sir Robert Lorimer with a vaulted plaster ceiling in the manner of the seventeenth century.

LEFT Turnpike stairhead with a thistle motif executed by Thomas Hadden.

problem. Observing that in wet weather the hall's fireplace wall ran with water, he enlisted numerous experts to solve the conundrum. After years of various experiments – one even advocated a complete rebuild of the west tower – the problem was solved when the tower was cocooned in polythene for a year and then covered in a protective layer of silicone. Many conservationists with their characteristic purist tenets have consistently urged Dr Joffe to reharl the tower, but this would be prohibitively expensive, and besides he likes the rough-hewn appearance of the exposed stonework, which adds considerably to the picturesquely rugged appearance appropriate to a tower standing guard over a Scottish loch.

NOTES

DUNDERAVE

130 Oliver Hill, *Scottish Castles of the 16th & 17th Centuries*, Country Life, 1953, p. 53

131 Ibid.

132 Christopher Hussey, *The Work of Sir Robert Lorimer*, Country Life, 1931

133 Ibid.

RIVINGTON CASTLE

LANCASHIRE

Tumbledown Rivington Castle, near Horwich in Lancashire, 7 miles/11 kilometres from Bolton on a flank of the West Pennines, is just below the 1,000-feet/305-metre contour. From it one can look up to the well-known Lancastrian landmark Beacon Tower, an early eighteenth-century eye-catcher on top of Rivington Pike, on the edge of Rivington Moor. The clearly deliberately ruinous construction is an intriguing puzzle. Built with thick blocks of ashlar and millstone grit, the local Pennine sandstone, the ruins simply do not have the delicacy of an eighteenth-century sham castle built as an eye-catcher. This deeply eccentric edifice is a little-known legacy of the Victorian titan Lord Leverhulme (1851–1925), begun in 1912.

'One associates such a quaint exercise as the building of a ruin with America rather than England,' wrote his son, 'and amongst Englishmen Lever was one of the few men – perhaps the only man – whom one can imagine carrying out such a scheme.'[134] Leverhulme had a passion for building. His architectural tastes were extensive, encompassing many different styles – Tudor, Jacobean, Queen Anne, Edwardian, Neoclassical Revival – which are reflected in his multitudinous architectural projects and homes. He and his

LEFT Lord Leverhulme, painted by Augustus John.

RIGHT Rivington Castle is planned around a large central courtyard.

LEFT The deliberate semi-ruinous state of Rivington Castle, as built by Lord Leverhulme, is shown in a selection of details.

wife lived in no fewer than thirteen houses during their marriage. On more than one occasion, he expressed a wish to have been an architect. 'He always entered into the design process, even preparing sketch plans himself' for all his building projects. On his death, Francis d'Arcy Cooper said that he was 'probably now arguing with St. Peter about the architecture of the gates'.[135]

William Hesketh Lever, created 1st Viscount Leverhulme of Bolton-le-Moors in 1917, was a remarkable figure both for his unstinting energy – he rose daily at 4.30 a.m. after sleeping outside in all weathers – and for his brilliant business acumen: from the wholesale family grocery business started by his father he created Lever Brothers, now Unilever.

In 1884, Lever and his brother James Darcy Lever decided to specialize in the manufacture of soap, setting up their own firm in Warrington. William was the driving force behind the firm's rapid success. He revolutionized the way soap was sold, dispensing with the traditional method of chopping it for the customer into slabs from a long line; instead the soap was cut at source and packaged in cardboard cartons emblazoned with the Sunlight logo – an extremely early example of product branding. The first batches rolled off the production line in January 1886; by the end of 1888 more than 14,000 tons a week were being produced.

Like many Victorian industrialists, Lord Leverhulme had a strongly developed philanthropic streak, and despite his prodigious success and ensuing wealth, he remained fiercely loyal to his Bolton origins throughout his life. Lever Park, in which Rivington Castle stands, is testimony to his munificence and far-sightedness. In 1899, hearing that the owners of Rivington Park, as it was then called, were in financial straits, Lever made a £40,000 bid for it, realizing the enormous potential it had as a much needed sylvan public park just a tram ride away from Bolton on the edge of wild moorland country. It extended from

Rivington Pike to reservoirs owned by Liverpool Corporation. The owners, the Crompton family, intimated that they wanted £70,000. At this juncture Liverpool Corporation entered the negotiations offering £50,000. This bid was rejected and eventually Lever secured a settlement for £60,000.

Leverhulme, naturally, saw the estate as yet another exciting building opportunity and he employed his greatest friend, the architect Jonathan Simpson (1850–1937), and his son, James Lomax-Simpson (1882–1977), also an architect (and later a director of Lever Brothers), to design many of the buildings that adorn Lever Park.

The overall vision for the 45-acre/18-hectare park – the terracing, huge lawns, ponds, pergolas, shelters, Japanese gardens, waterfalls and loggias – was the result of a fruitful partnership between Lever and the landscape designer Thomas Mawson (1861–1933), later President of the Town Planning Institute. Mawson described both site and client as 'exceptional'.[136] 'Of all Lord Leverhulme's building activities, those at Rivington grip the imagination most. His gardens on their vast and precipitous hillside site are amongst his most memorable works, and which in their present, partially ruined, forgotten state create a highly romantic and sublime impression.'[137]

There is an undated and unsigned perspective by Mawson of Rivington Castle in the Mawson archive in Kendal, but James Lomax-Simpson in conversation with Michael Shippobottom in the 1970s claimed it as his design. Shippobottom suggests that Lomax-Simpson was the site architect.[138]

Rivington Castle is a full-scale conjectural reconstruction, deliberately built in a ruinous state, of Liverpool Castle, which was built in the thirteenth century and badly damaged in the Civil War. Its demolition to make room for better traffic access to the city in 1720 was an early example of brutal town planning. It is thought that Lever was inspired to reconstruct it after reading 'An attempt to Recover the Plans of the Castle of Liverpool' by Edward Cox in Volume 42 of *The Transactions of the Historic Society of Lancashire and Cheshire*, published in 1890. Lever was a member of the society. Lever apparently saw a resemblance between the castle's site and the area to the side of Rivington Reservoir.

The castle stands at the apex of three avenues overlooking Rivington Reservoir and is built around a courtyard plan, similar to that of Bolingbroke Castle in Lincolnshire. Irregular in layout, it has a curtain wall, drum towers in the corners, roofless rooms, a spiral staircase and seemingly crumbling parapets. On close investigation the ruin reveals amusing conceits: for instance, the thinnest of corridors leads to a minuscule room, a flight of steps ascends to nothing and there are random corbels that have never supported anything.

The original intention was to open a tea garden in the inner ward. According to Leverhulme's son, work on the castle started in 1912; it was still under construction in 1916 but remained unfinished at the time of his death in 1925 and remains so to this day. The catalogue of the 1925 sale of the estate following his death refers to construction equipment still being on site. It also refers to a 'model of Liverpool Castle in a mahogany, square case, glazed top and sides, on four cabriole legs 15 and a half inches square, 42 inches high'.

As a bold experiment in landscape design Rivington Castle has certainly succeeded. 'Future generations will be grateful for this careful reconstruction of a piece of bygone Liverpool,' wrote Lord Leverhulme's son, the 2nd Viscount, in 1927, adding, 'Already the newness is wearing off, and it will not be long before Nature has speckled the stones with lichen, filled the crannies with moss, and paved the courtyard with grass so that the uninitiated will not know that the replica is not a genuine ruin.'[139]

He would be saddened to learn that today the castle, now owned by United Utilities, is forlorn and at the time of writing has been closed after vandalism. 'Yobs on rampage at castle ruins' ran a story in the *Bolton News* in November 2010.

NOTES

RIVINGTON CASTLE

134 W.H.L. Leverhulme (2nd Viscount), *Viscount Leverhulme*, George Allen & Unwin, 1927, p. 131

135 Matthew Hyde and Michael Shippobottom, notes for a Victorian Society Manchester Group visit to Bolton and Rivington, 15 July 2006

136 Michael Shippobottom, 'Unmatched for Drama', *Country Life*, 13 August 1984, p. 678

137 Matthew Hyde and Michael Shippobottom, notes for a Victorian Society Manchester Group visit to Bolton and Rivington, 15 July 2006

138 Letter from Michael Shippobottom to Amicia de Moubray, 5 August 2009

139 W.H.L. Leverhulme (2nd Viscount), *Viscount Leverhulme*, George Allen & Unwin, 1927

LEFT Above: Looking from Rivington Castle up to Beacon Tower on top of Rivington Pike in the far distance. Below: The ivy-covered ruins overlook Rivington Reservoir.

EILEAN DONAN
ROSS-SHIRE

One of the most beautifully situated of all Scottish castles, its fortified silhouette rising up out of an island in the middle of a loch set against the backdrop of the mountains of Kintail, Eilean Donan is the epitome of a stirring Scottish castle. It has become an iconic image of Scotland and can be found adorning every kind of Scottish souvenir from shortbread tins to calendars. Numerous films, including *Goldeneye* and *Highlander*, have used it as a location.

Of the many thousands of visitors the castle attracts each year from all over the world, probably very few realize at first that most of what they are gazing at is less than a century old. For Eilean Donan, like Duart Castle further down the western seaboard, is not an ancient castle but an early twentieth-century picturesque reincarnation of one.

Eilean Donan, or 'island of Donan', is probably named after the sixth-century Irish saint Bishop Donan, who alighted in Scotland in about 580. Strategically situated at the confluence of three sea lochs, Loch Donan, Loch Duich and Loch Alsh, and on the principal east–west route across the Highlands to the Isle of Skye, it has played an important role in defending the west coast since time immemorial; and the castle built on it in medieval times acted as an important defensive structure in an area where the sea was the sole thoroughfare for warring clan chieftains. Alexander III gave the lands to Colin Fitzgerald, son of the Irish Earl of Desmond and Kildare, for his help in defeating King Hakkon and his Norsemen at the Battle of Largs in 1263. In 1331 Randolph, Earl of Moray, executed fifty men at Eilean Donan and adorned the castle walls with their severed heads. In 1539 the castle was besieged by Donald Gorm MacDonald, a claimant to the Lordships of the Isles. He was killed by a single arrow shot from the castle.

The castle today is much smaller than the original one, which occupied the whole island. In the fifteenth century, for reasons unknown, the castle was drastically reduced, only one tower being left standing at the island's highest point. So it remained until 1719, when it was attacked by three government frigates, which blew the Jacobite-supporting garrison of forty-six Spanish soldiers asunder. Captain Herman of the *Enterprise* went ashore to accept the surrender and detonate the powder magazine, which promptly exploded, blasting the castle to smithereens.

LEFT Eilean Donan Castle, recreated 1913–32 for Major John MacRae-Gilstrap.

The desolate remains served as a poignant reminder of the violent Jacobite rebellion and were abandoned for the next 193 years until they fired the imagination of Major John MacRae-Gilstrap (1861–1937), the second son of the MacRae family of nearby Conchra.

Deputy Hereditary Keeper of the Palace of Holyrood House, a member of the Honourable Corps of Gentleman at Arms and of the Royal Company of Archers, the King's Bodyguard for Scotland, Macrae-Gilstrap clearly delighted in public duty and historical honorary offices. He was much taken with the role as the hereditary constable of Eilean Donan of his forebear, Christopher MacRae, and that of the latter's son, Farquhar MacRae, the last constable and owner of Eilean Donan, who

was born there in 1580 and lived 'in an opulent and flourishing condition, much given to hospitality and charity'.[140]

In 1912 MacRae-Gilstrap bought Eilean Donan from Sir Keith Fraser of Inverinate. Negotiations must have been somewhat protracted, as the particulars of sale were available in 1907 but it was not until 1910 that Francis Grant at the Lyon Office wrote to MacRae applauding him for purchasing 'such a historical place connected with your family' and advising him to convene 'a gathering of the Clan to take formal possession'.[141] The receipt issued by Macrae-Gilstrap's Edinburgh solicitors for his cheque for £2,500, being the payment for the castle, is dated January 1913.

In August 1913, Macrae-Gilstrap must have been thrilled

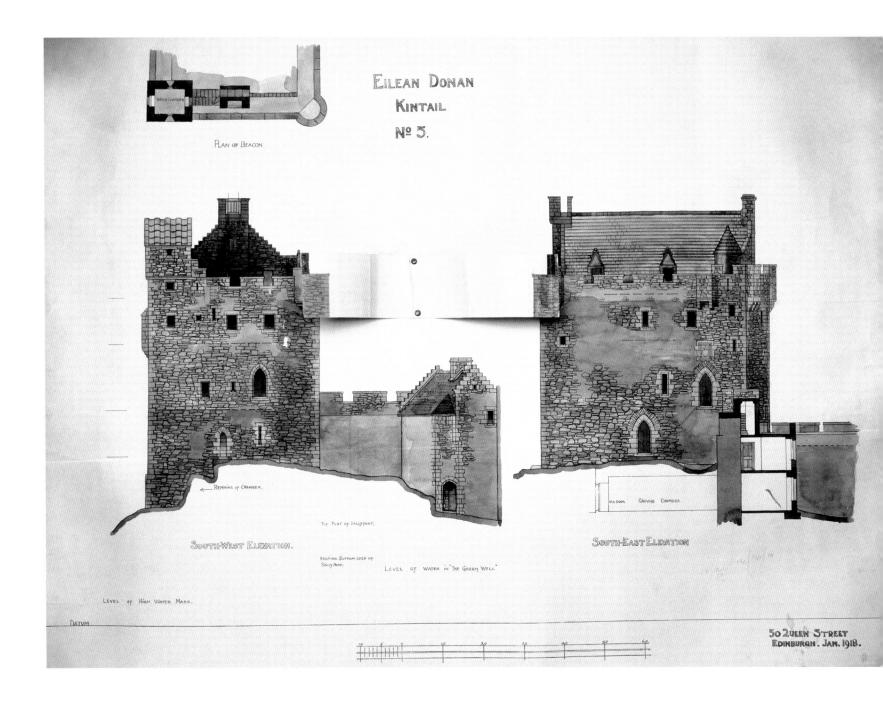

EILEAN DONAN
KINTAIL
Nº 5.

PLAN OF BEACON

REMAINS OF CHAMBER.

Top Plat of Sallyport.

SOUTH-WEST ELEVATION.

Existing Bottom Step of
Sally Port.

LEVEL OF WATER IN "THE GREEN WELL"

SOUTH-EAST ELEVATION

OLD DOOR.   GROUND CHAMBER.

LEVEL OF HIGH WATER MARK.

DATUM

50 QUEEN STREET
EDINBURGH. JAN. 1918.

when an impressive clan gathering numbering more than three hundred, headed by the late Edward VII's piper, marched to the castle, and Duncan MacRae triumphantly unfurled his father's banner as constable of Ellandona, 'thus linking the present with the romantic days of old'.[142]

MacRae-Gilstrap had married a wealthy heiress, Isabella Mary Gilstrap, in 1889. Second daughter and co-heiress of George Gilstrap, she was also co-heiress of her uncle, Sir William Gilstrap, Bt, of Fornham Park, Suffolk, head of a successful malting business, Gilstrap Earp and Co. On Sir William's death in 1896, as a condition of inheritance Captain MacRae (as he then was) assumed the Gilstrap surname. Happily his wife encouraged him in his ambitions, stumping up £250,000 towards the purchase and restoration of the castle and even later writing *The Clan MacRae*.

In MacRae's widely reported speech at the opening ceremony he expressed his hope that 'part of [the castle] at least might rise from its ruins'.[143] He set to work at once, employing a local clansman, Farquhar MacRae, who dedicated the next twenty years to the project and is said to have foreseen the appearance of the rebuilt castle in a dream.

OPPOSITE Eilean Donan was abandoned after being shelled by English men-of-war in 1719.

ABOVE George Mackie Watson's detailed drawings for the restoration.

PREVIOUS PAGES Eilean
Donan is strategically located for
defensive purposes where three
sea lochs meet on the main east–
west route across the Highlands to
the Isle of Skye.

BELOW The rubble causeway and
bridge linking the island to the
mainland was built in 1932.

CANDIDE FORTITUDINE SECURE
1912
NEC·CURO·NEC·CAREO

CHO FAD'S A BHIOS MACRATH A STIGH
CHA BHI FRISEALACH A MUIGH.

JMᶜRG 1928

EMᶜRG 1928

LEFT The MacRae-Gilstrap coat of arms above the portcullis.

Before departing for the First World War in the splendid style of a clan chief (he raised and commanded the 11th Battalion of Royal Highlanders), Major MacRae-Gilstrap engaged George Mackie Watson (1860–1948), a little-known Edinburgh architect who had worked as an assistant to Sir Rowan Anderson on the Scottish National Portrait Gallery and on the Major's estate at Ballimore, as well as at Conchra.

The re-creation is very much in the spirit of a picturesque revival, playing on a beguilingly dream-like image of a medieval castle and largely eschewing the austere aesthetic of many traditional Scottish castles. The Major undertook prodigious research in pursuit of visual references to the appearance of the original fort, writing to museums, antiquarian societies and galleries. The main tower is a rebuilding of the fourteenth-

century tower house. Only the south part of the L-plan block was rebuilt as an austere crow-stepped house. The south-east building was altered and extended. Watson gave full rein to picturesque licence, greatly elaborating the entrance gateway with a working portcullis and adding machicolations, bartizans, gothic-style windows, a sea gate and, despite the exposed position, unharled rubble walls and a three-arched bridge to the mainland. The ultimate romantic twist was achieved by lowering the original level of the courtyard to expose the bare bedrock of the island, creating the impression that the castle has grown out of the ground.

Roughly hewn steps lead up from the courtyard into a tunnel-vaulted billeting room on the ground floor of the keep; upstairs are the banqueting hall and secret passages

and spy-holes, pithily described by John Gifford as 'a rubbly Edwardian stage-set for life in the Middle Ages'.[144] The hefty Douglas fir ceiling beams in the banqueting hall were a gift from the MacRaes of Canada and were shipped from British Columbia. The aim was to combine modern conveniences – electric light and central heating – with the honest (non-machine-made) simulation of antiquity.

The project was fraught with difficulties because of the location. Quarried stones weighing up to 30cwt from the nearby hills could only be got on to the site by being 'dragged by a horse to the shore, and there, at low tide, chained to the bottom of a boat, which when the tide rose, was rowed over to the castle'.[145] Hewn oak beams, steel stanchions and green

slates from Caithness came by train from Edinburgh to Kyle of Lochalsh, by road to Ardelve and by boat to the island. It proved too aggravating to be dependent on the tides for getting on and off the island, and in 1932 a rubble causeway and bridge linking the island to the mainland was built as the final link between the mainland and the Major's conceit.

Sadly MacRae died four months short of the re-created castle's official opening in July 1932, attended by several hundred MacRaes and representatives of other clans, all wearing Highland dress. Lord Lovat performed the opening ceremony. The MacRaes' descendants still have a flat in the castle, which they use for holidays. It is been open to the public since 1960 and annually attracts thousands of visitors.

OPPOSITE The banqueting hall on the first floor of the keep has secret passages and spy-holes.

ABOVE The billeting room on the ground floor of the keep. The barrel-vaulted ceiling is 2½ feet/ 75 centimetres thick at the centre.

NOTES

EILEAN DONAN
140 Article in *The Scots Pictorial*, 18 June 1921, p. 608
141 Antony Woodward, 'Eilean Donan', *Country Life*, 31 January 1994, p. 50
142 Article in *The Scots Pictorial*, 18 June 1921, p. 608
143 *Country Life*, 13 January 1994
144 John Gifford, *Highlands and Islands* (Pevsner Architectural Guides: Buildings of Scotland), Yale University Press, 1992
145 *The Times*, 18 July 1932

ALICK.P.F.RITCHIE.

"Self —"

GORDON SELFRIDGE'S CASTLE
HAMPSHIRE

'Build me the biggest castle in the world,' Gordon Selfridge is believed to have instructed the architect Philip Tilden. The brilliant American retailer Selfridge was flush with the success of the world's first dedicated department store, which he opened in London in 1909; he liked to boast that, after Westminster Abbey and the Tower of London, his store was the third biggest tourist attraction in town. He was a man of wildly extravagant tastes whose architectural ambitions knew no bounds, even during the depths of the First World War.

Harry Gordon Selfridge was born in Ripon, Wisconsin, in 1856. He began his career as personal assistant to the retail manager of Marshall Field in Chicago in 1885. He quickly showed an astute understanding of retailing by persuading Field to hold twice-yearly 'mark-down sales' and to open a bargain basement. Within two years he was general manager of the store.

Following Marshall Field's death in 1906 at the age of fifty, Selfridge bravely decided to move to London. Three years later, on 15 March 1909, he opened Selfridges, thus changing the art of retailing for ever. More than a million people poured into the store in its first week. Selfridge himself became an object of curiosity. 'There was always a small crowd waiting outside to see him arrive at work each morning at 8.30 a.m. An observer recalled that "he was received in respectable silence by the bystanders who always waved at him."'[146]

Sir Martin Conway introduced Selfridge to Philip Tilden over lunch at the Ritz in 1917. Selfridge immediately instructed Tilden to design a 450-foot/137-metre tower to grace the top of the store, which was doing well: profits in 1917 were £258,000 (more than £10 million today). But Selfridge had to contend with five years of battling with the Portman Estates and Marylebone Council before he got permission to build the tower. According to the *Evening Standard* he justified the tower by saying, 'A store used every day should be as ennobling a thing as a church or as a museum. I love to look at a beautiful building.' Tilden produced several different schemes but the project never came to fruition. 'Forget it, forget it,' retorted Selfridge when a journalist asked him about the future of the tower.[147]

Selfridge paid Tilden a retainer for his work and this meant that Tilden was at Selfridge's behest for any amount of routine meetings. 'The two men formed a close relationship; Tilden later recorded how impressed he had been by the magnitude of [Selfridge's] imaginative thoughts';[148] Selfridge even took Tilden on holiday to Spain with his son.

LEFT *Vanity Fair* Spy cartoon of Harry Gordon Selfridge.

A brash, bold, impulsive and imaginative character, in 1916 Selfridge took a £5,000-a-year lease on Highcliffe Castle in Hampshire, a Gothic Revival country house designed between 1831 and 1832 by William Donthorn for Lord Stuart de Rothesay. Over the next six years Selfridge spent vast amounts of money on modernizing it in keeping with his unrestrained lifestyle, installing bathrooms, steam central heating and modern kitchens. Highcliffe Castle looks out over Hengistbury Head, a ravishing headland with superb views over to the Isle of Wight. When his neighbour Sir George Meyrick put the headland up for sale in 1930, Selfridge snapped it up and that was when he instructed Tilden to draw up plans for a vast castle.

The local community viewed the scheme with alarm, particularly as Hengistbury Head is recognized as one of the most important Bronze Age archaeological sites in Europe. Metallurgical finds (more than three thousand coins) made in 1915 were deemed to be the most important yet in Britain, providing evidence of extensive human habitation from the fourth century BC to around 100 BC. Rumours circulated: Selfridge was thought to be planning to build a factory or even a Wild West park, despite his promise to Christchurch Town Council that he would work with archaeologists during the construction and take steps to prevent erosion of the Head and always allow public access. In a philanthropic vein, Selfridge planned to rent space at Hengistbury Head to artists who, he hoped, would produce fine work inspired by their magnificent surroundings.

Tilden writes at length about the plans for the castle in his autobiography, *True Remembrances*. 'The plan . . . was immense: it was a great and glorified dream. The only way

LEFT Perspective view by Philip Tilden of the proposed castle and promontory at Hengistbury Head, Hampshire.

RIGHT Philip Tilden (1887–1956) in the 1920s in the hall at Wardes, Kent.

in which I could get it all on a sheet of paper was to make it to sixty-fourth scale, and then to develop it in bits.'[149] Tilden made a monthly visit to Selfridge to present him with the latest drawings, sometimes at the Oxford Street store and sometimes at Highcliffe, where he liked to surround himself with fellow retail magnates such as Sir Thomas Lipton and Sir Ernest Cassel.

The scheme, which was for a huge castle with a smaller private house below, was of a magnitude suitable for a fabulously wealthy Indian maharajah. Agnes Conway recorded in her diary that it was going to cost £2–2.5 million.[150] There was to be a dual drive through a gateway in a bastioned wall, 'like the gate to a Spanish city . . . The drives gradually drifted apart, the secondary one deferentially, at a slightly lower plane, to lead to the lower level of the house, and the upper rising higher until it entered an immense turning place, rather in the manner of some piazza in Rome, accentuated by fountain, grass and stone walk. At this upper level, there were to be three entrances: firstly, to the theatre, picture galleries, tennis courts and baths; secondly, to the very centre of the

whole creation and thirdly, to a mighty tower to rise so big and high that it would dominate the countryside as far as the eye could see. The whole plan was strung on one great vista, more than a thousand feet long, and widening centrally at the main entry. The hall of this was to be domed, and from its marble floor wide sweeping stairs were to rise and hide themselves in a hundred arches on either hand where galleries led forth in diverse directions.'[151] The diameter of the proposed tower, which would have been visible far out at sea, only 10 feet/3 metres less than the dome of St Paul's Cathedral, gives an idea of the fantastical scale of the whole edifice.

There were to be at least 250 suites of rooms for guests, each with its own bedroom, dressing room, bathroom and sitting room; as well as several drawing rooms overlooking a vast winter garden, dining rooms capable of seating hundreds, a *galerie des glaces* as at Versailles, and elaborate cloistered gardens, including a winter garden.

When Selfridge was asked, '"How will you ever get it done? Or how big did you say it was?" his response was to eye his

interrogators with a rather cold, clear, blue and calculating eye, thrusting out his chin without a glimmer of a smile.' According to the *Building News* in 1923, he merely 'intended the building as an imaginative exercise and never proposed erecting it'.[152] A close friend, Ralph Blumenfield, the editor of the *Daily Express*, wrote in his diary, 'he plans to build a wonderful castellated palace which shall be the most beautiful architectural effort of modern history'. Blumenfield's boss, the proprietor Lord Beaverbrook, believed it would 'remain in the region of dreams'.[153] Not surprisingly it did: the plans remained a castle in the air.

Tilden executed literally hundreds and hundreds of drawings for a monthly presentation to Selfridge. The last extant drawing is dated 1922. Mr Mabey made a 'beautiful small plaster model of the castle at the end of the headland'. 'I spent many an hour with Mr. Mabey, adjusting, correcting and enjoying the making of this meticulous creation.'[154] Philip Tilden waited for the go-ahead but it never came. Five years of discussion and plans came to nothing.

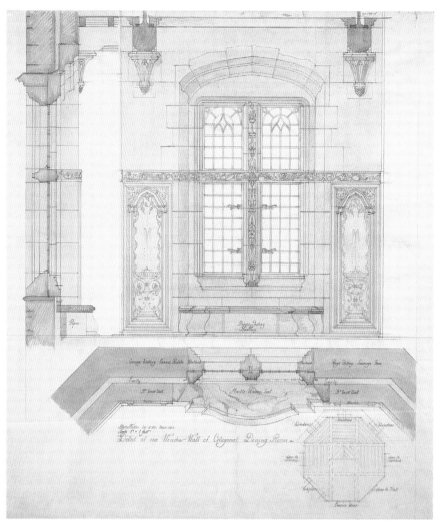

Eventually in 1930 Selfridge put the estate up for sale. Yet again this provoked consternation amongst the locals, this time not because of the archaeological remains but because of the threat of encroaching suburbanization as a result of the site's proximity to the growing town of Bournemouth. Bournemouth Corporation organized a committee to visit Gordon Selfridge's agent, Sir Howard Frank, to see if he would negotiate with a public body to save the site 'becoming a bungalow town'.[155]

Happily, Selfridge agreed to sell it to the Corporation at a considerably reduced price. Eighty years on, it remains a popular beauty spot visited by thousands of people every year.

OPPOSITE Drawing by Philip Tilden of the castle as it would appear if seen from the sea.

ABOVE Sketches by Philip Tilden for a mirror (left) and a window (right).

NOTES

GORDON SELFRIDGE'S CASTLE
146 Lindy Woodhead, *Shopping and Seduction and Mr. Selfridge*, Profile Books, 2008, p. 90
147 Ibid., p. 154
148 Ibid.
149 Philip Tilden, *True Remembrances: The Memoirs of an Architect*, Country Life, 1954
150 James Bettley, notes made 27 July 1981 for *Lush and Luxurious: The Life of Philip Tilden*, RIBA, 1987
151 Philip Tilden, *True Remembrances: The Memoirs of an Architect*, Country Life, 1954, pp. 54–5
152 *Building News*, 1923
153 Reginald Pound, *Selfridge*, Heinemann, 1960
154 Philip Tilden, *True Remembrances: The Memoirs of an Architect*, Country Life, 1954, p. 58
155 *The Times*, 24 April 1930

ST DONAT'S CASTLE
GLAMORGANSHIRE

'Want buy castle in England' read the terse wire the American newspaper tycoon Randolph Hearst sent to his English agent, Alice Head. Hearst, the son of George Hearst, a self-made millionaire miner and ranch owner who left him $18 million, was an American business magnate and the creator of a chain of newspapers across the United States. And he had casually dropped into conversation at a dinner with Alice Head earlier that year in New York that if St Donat's or Leeds Castle ever came on the market, he should be told. In 1910 he established the National Magazine Company in England. As a child he was reputed to have told his mother that he would like to live at Windsor Castle. He rejected Leeds Castle after Miss Head wired him: 'Made thorough inspection

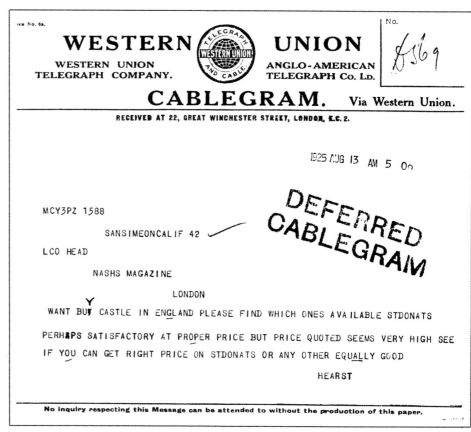

LEFT Aerial view of St Donat's Castle, Glamorganshire, showing the 150-foot-long swimming pool in the foreground.

LEFT Randolph Hearst at
St Donat's Castle.

RIGHT The medieval gatehouse.

Leeds Castle last Saturday stop Quite unique as antiquity but needs expenditure large sum to make it habitable not a bath in place only lighting oil lamps servants quarters down dungeons and in steep battlemented towers stop Part could be made fit to live in by spending about four thousand.'

On seeing St Donat's in Glamorganshire advertised for sale in *Country Life* in 1925, on 12 August Miss Head wired Hearst: 'Period place in excellent repair with central heating modern sanitation.' To this he replied: 'Buy St Donat's.' 'It [the telegram] was on my desk one morning, so I just bought it. I didn't communicate with him anymore.'[156] Hearst paid £130,000, a figure which Head described 'as nothing' to him. It became Hearst's – or strictly the National Magazine Company's – in October. It seems extraordinary that it was bought sight unseen. The identity of the purchaser quickly leaked out. Miss Head grumbles in a letter to the solicitor about 'a terrible week warding off reporters', ending 'Mr. Hearst is keener about this Castle than anything he has ever bought.'[157]

St Donat's was a much more attractive proposition than Leeds, in that it had already been sensitively restored at the beginning of the century by Morgan Williams, a noted Welsh antiquarian who also owned a celebrated collection of armour and early furniture. 'It is a large and curious old place and will require considerable study before making up one's mind as to what should be done with as little as possible with the structure,'[158] Morgan Williams wrote to the architect Thomas Garner, asking if he would undertake the work. The resulting restoration was praised by H. Avray Tipping in *Country Life*: 'Most fortunate is the result to those lovers of old-world fabrics and old-world ways who are able to feel themselves almost transported back to medieval times when they are admitted through the ancient gate-house and restored curtain walls.'[159]

What would he have thought of Elinor Glyn's description of staying at St Donat's just over twenty years later? 'Into the thick castle walls he [Hearst] had built dozens of new bathrooms and decorated them lavishly with genuine medieval tapestries

and suits of armours. Downstairs gramophones blared and minor film stars shrieked; and presiding over everything was the genial but autocratic figure of Hearst himself, resplendent in bright pink tie and Tyrolean hat.' As for the guests, 'they play [Monopoly] all night . . . The boredom of it! And not even for money.'[160]

Hearst did not visit St Donat's until September 1928, at the end of a Continental tour, and even then it was a fleeting visit of less than twenty-four hours. Nevertheless, driven there by the indefatigable Miss Head, with typical brio he raced round all the 135 rooms before dinner and left for Southampton the next morning to sail back to America.

Hearst's entourage included his mistress, Marion Davies, and the architect Sir Charles Allom (1865–1947). The character Charles Foster Kane in the film *Citizen Kane* is modelled on Hearst and when Orson Welles, as Kane, tells his mistress, 'This is our home,' the parallel to St Donat's is evident. 'The "home" was Xanadu, a megalomaniac dream castle of gargantuan proportions.'[161]

Hearst probably met Allom through the art dealer Joseph Duveen, from whom he bought pictures. Allom, founder of White Allom and Co. (of London, Montreal and New York), had recently finished redecorating Buckingham Palace, for which he was knighted. Allom was the favourite choice of Anglo-American clients in the US who wanted the English interior style, including Henry Clay Frick. Within weeks, Sir Charles Allom had received a twenty-five-page letter from Hearst outlining in great detail his plans for overhauling the castle and bringing it up to date with every modern convenience and luxury.

For Hearst St Donat's was a wonderful opportunity to use some of his existing collection as well as an excuse to purchase more. He was avaricious in his pursuit of architectural salvages of every style and date. '"Collecting" implies acquisition with a collection in mind, but so mind-blowing was the scale of his purchases, so diverse and unequal in quality, so grotesque the utter lack of self-discipline, that his motivation, beyond the lust for acquisitions, is baffling.'[162] A typical cable sent in

1924 to Miss Head reads: 'Are there any important ceilings to be had in England also staircases of Tudor or Jacobean period would like one trussed ceiling of guildhall type.'[163]

In all more than two hundred salvaged bits and pieces, including twenty-two fireplaces, were incorporated. 'Hearst's imports are a product of his "fall guy" mania for buying anything and everything offered by the antiques trade.'[164] His flagrant disdain for architectural purity is demonstrated by the manner in which fireplaces were ruthlessly cut down to fit at St Donat's or even made up of an assortment of pieces – hood and frieze supported on jambs from a different piece. Many of the rooms present an extraordinary jigsaw of different salvage trophies of various dates. For example, the banqueting hall boasts a late medieval Valois fireplace

from Beauvais as well as a late gothic screen from a house in Bridgewater, Somerset.

A particularly controversial issue was the dismantling of Bradenstoke Priory, Wiltshire. In 1929 the medieval tithe barn was taken down stone by stone amid great secrecy; the workmen did not even know who was employing them. The western range of the cloister, including the prior's lodging and the refectory, soon followed. Understandably, the defilement of Bradenstoke became a cause célèbre in the annals of the Society for the Protection of Ancient Buildings. 'The grossest imaginable violation of the Society's principles,' Ralph Edwards of the Victoria and Albert Museum wrote. 'How any self-respecting firm of London decorators . . . could ever have brought themselves to do such a thing is incomprehensible.'[165]

OPPOSITE The armoury.

LEFT The great hall and its
oriel recess, showing some of
Morgan Williams's fine collection
of armour, photographed for
Country Life 1907.

Questions were even asked in Parliament.

The splendid fourteenth-century double collar-beam roof was fitted into a specially devised hall at St Donat's. In a further act of 'vandalism' part of the outer curtain wall was demolished to accommodate it and windows from the prior's lodgings were built into the walls. The outraged SPAB mounted a national campaign, sticking up posters in the Tube showing before and after photographs.

Thus Hearst transformed the castle into a plutocrat's palace, overlaid with romantic connotations, in which to entertain his international guests. The thirty-two new bathrooms put such demand on the existing reservoir that a water main was laid from Bridgend some 9 miles/14.5 kilometres distant. The engineer from the South Wales Electricity Power Company was astonished to be asked for connections for all manner of cutting-edge electrical gadgets including private hairdressing apparatus, electric clocks and thermostatic controls. His other clients in the area were still wary of electricity, limiting themselves to a solitary light in the middle of rooms.

Christie's had dispersed Morgan Williams's superb collection of armour in a two-day sale in 1921, described as of 'especial attraction to the connoisseur.'[166] Hearst set out to create 'the most comprehensive collection of arms and armour',[167] poaching a Frenchman, Raymond Bartel, from the Armoury Department of the Metropolitan Museum of Art to assemble it. For the next twenty-one years Bartel scoured Europe, putting together a collection described by *Connoisseur* magazine as 'astonishing'.[168]

At that time it was relatively easy to accumulate a fine collection of antique furniture, as the twelve-volume photographic inventory of St Donat's testifies. Some of the furniture was bought on merit, some for its historical associations. Hearst slept in a bed reputed to have been slept in by Charles I. The frenzied shopping that Hearst indulged in sometimes resulted in objects being shunted around hither and thither, as when a collection of beds – Jacobean, Hepplewhite and Chippendale – was shipped to America and then back to St Donat's.

It is tempting to think that Anthony Powell modelled Sir Magnus Donner, the immensely rich industrialist and patron of the arts who buys Stourwater Castle from a landed family in Powell's twelve-volume sequence *A Dance to the Music of Time*, on Randolph Hearst and St Donat's Castle, as there are many similarities. His description of the interiors, replete with tapestries and armour, could easily have been of St Donat's during Hearst's ownership.

For twelve years St Donat's was Hearst's European home. Accompanied by Marion Davies, he visited it five times for a total occupation just short of four months. Guests were met at Cardiff station by a fleet of Buicks, Studebakers and Packards, all sporting the stars and stripes on each fender. Winston Churchill, George Bernard Shaw, Charlie Chaplin, Clark Gable, Errol Flynn, Ivor Novello, Jack Kennedy, the Mountbattens and David Lloyd George were among the guests. To entertain them Hearst drafted in chefs from the Savoy and Claridge's and installed tennis courts and a huge swimming pool, measuring 150 x 50 feet/46 x 15 metres, filled with purified sea water and with underwater lighting. Mercifully, and showing a rare streak of empathy with the *genius loci*, apart from building a little Italian summerhouse with a telephone from which to call his editors, he did not tamper with the fine terraced gardens descending to the shore with far-reaching views over the Bristol Channel.

As Hearst lost the control of his empire, he was forbidden to visit St Donat's in case it later incurred death duties. The castle was put up for sale in 1938. The National Magazine Company found itself encumbered with an unwanted albatross. It consulted a solicitor, Major Milner, the Deputy Speaker at the House of Commons. His opinion was: 'Only one man might be able to use the premises to good advantage. That man is a Mr. Butlin, a Canadian, who has a chain of holiday camps throughout the British Isles and who has

amassed a tremendous fortune from these operations . . . The consensus is that we have at St. Donat's a white elephant of the rarest species, and that Mr. Hearst should be prevailed upon to authorise the disposal of the premises without delay in view of the fact that in no circumstances will he be able to occupy them short of three years.'[169]

In 1940 the castle was requisitioned as an officers' training centre. Some time after the Second World War there was a plan to set up a girls' domestic science college under the auspices of *Good Housekeeping* but this came to nothing. In 1959 a Welsh property developer tried to get planning permission to develop the site as a caravan park and holiday camp. Fortunately this was turned down and the next year M. Antonin Besse, son of the founder of St Antony's College, Oxford, donated the castle and the estate to the United World College of the Atlantic, which remains there to this day.

NOTES

ST DONAT'S CASTLE

156 Enfys McMurry, *Hearst's Other Castle,* Seren, 1999, p. 15
157 Ibid.
158 Morgan Williams to Thomas Garner, 13 August 1901
159 H. Avray Tipping, 'St. Donat's Castle', *Country Life,* 31 August 1907, p. 315
160 Anthony Glyn, *Elinor Glyn,* Hutchinson, 1955, p. 322
161 Clive Aslet, *The Last Country Houses,* Yale University Press, 1982
162 John Harris, *Moving Rooms: The Trade in Architectural Salvage,* Yale University Press, 2007, p. 219
163 Clive Aslet, *The Last Country Houses,* Yale University Press, 1982
164 Ibid., p.85
165 Enfys McMurry, *Hearst's Other Castle,* Seren, 1999, p. 35
166 *Country Life,* 2 April 1921
167 Enfys McMurry, *Hearst's Other Castle,* Seren, 1999
168 Ibid., p. 49
169 Clive Aslet, *The Last Country Houses,* Yale University Press, 1982

OPPOSITE The castle from the watch tower, looking east.

LEFT The rose garden was laid out as a Tudor heraldic garden by Morgan Williams.

SALTWOOD CASTLE
KENT

'Saltwood Castle should be as well known to the public, capturing its errant imagination as much, as Kenilworth or Carnarvon, but no man has embroidered its story into popular literature,' wrote the architect Philip Tilden.[170] A couple of miles from Lympne Castle (see page 40), Saltwood Castle, near Hythe, Kent, is today probably best known as the home of the flamboyant late Alan Clark, MP. But the notoriety of which Tilden writes was as the setting for the plotting of the murder of Thomas Becket in 1170. Five knights – Randulf de Broc, Reginald FitzUrse, Hugh de Moreville, William Tracy and Richard le Bret – sat up long into the night of 28 December in a vaulted chamber at Saltwood, with their candles snuffed for fear of seeing each other's faces. The assassins returned there the next day, having accomplished the deed.

The castle is believed to stand on a Roman site. It is first recorded in a medieval manuscript relating to St John's Hospital in Hythe that Aesc, the son of Hengist and King of Kent, 'built a castle at this place' soon after his accession in 488. Set on a promontory between two streams on a bluff on which the port of Portus Lemanis stood, it was of strategic importance. In 833 by a charter of King Egbert it was granted to the church of St Mary at Lyminge, before it became a palace of the Archbishops of Canterbury.

The oldest parts of the castle still extant date from the twelfth and fourteenth centuries. The castle was severely damaged by an earthquake in 1580 and thereafter was abandoned for the next three hundred years. The castle is still occasionally damaged by small earthquakes.

Externally the gatehouse, with its twin castellated towers, is a copybook image of every child's fairytale castle. The entire outer portion, the present gateway and the round flanking towers stylistically belong to what is sometimes called the 'the twilight age of castles' – in the sense that aesthetic form had by then become a greater consideration than military defence.

The castle passed into the prominent local Deedes family in the eighteenth century but it was not until 1882 that any work on it was undertaken. William

LEFT The wall of the inner bailey is punctuated by medieval towers on a rectangular plan.

ABOVE Jane Clark, Lord Clark, Alan Clark, Andrew and James in front of Saltwood Castle.

Deedes restored and considerably added to the gatehouse, extending it on either side at the back with the help of the architect Frederick Beeston and making it habitable once again.

Life in a castle, however picturesque, is not always a romantic idyll, as the late Lord Deedes, a well-known journalist, recalled. His mother and his maiden aunts had persuaded his father to move from nearby Sandling Park into Saltwood when he was six years old. 'Young friends did not feel drawn to it or me. Water ran down the walls, there was no electricity or gas, and fires had to be lit in every room just to keep the damp at bay.'[171] The upkeep had a disastrous effect on the family's fortunes and Bill Deedes's father sold off large tranches of land. Ultimately both his mother's and one of his younger sisters' health suffered. It must have been a relief when Saltwood was eventually sold by the Deedes family in 1925, after the Wall Street crash, to Reginald and Iva Lawson, his family then being proprietors of the *Daily Telegraph*.

The Lawsons set about imposing their own character on the castle, spending vast sums in the process, deliberately trying to hide the then deeply unfashionable Victorian alterations that had been made principally to the rooms in the gatehouse.

A formidable but reclusive figure, Mrs Lawson's 'whole aim in life was to own castles'.[172] A couple of years after buying Saltwood, it is believed that she persuaded her husband to buy Herstmonceux Castle (see page 96). Tragically he shot himself in the woods at Saltwood a few months later.[173] After his death Iva threw herself into Saltwood. Lord Clark describes her: 'She had a passion for building, employing a resident mason full time: his restorations were harmless, partly because he was not very skilful. Mrs. Lawson personally supervised all the work and would arrive promptly on site at 8am every morning. If a piece of masonry looked insecure she would push it over with her foot.'[174]

RIGHT The south side of the inner bailey.

Mrs Lawson saw practically no one, but her passion for castles led her to visit Allington (see page 74), where she met Lord Conway and decided to add both him and his castle to her life. 'Don't faint', wrote Lord Conway to his sister, Minnie, 'I am going to marry Iva Lawson. Since her husband accidentally shot himself four years ago she has lived in complete retirement.'[175] Conway was soon living at Saltwood and at the age of seventy-eight, 'paunchy and almost blind',[176] he was inveigled by his new wife to do exercises on the lawn. Clark ascribes Conway's marriage to his being lonely: 'otherwise I cannot imagine how a man with so keen a sense of self-preservation could have taken such a suicidal step'.[177]

Philip Tilden, who had been the architect at Allington Castle, came in Conway's wake and soon R. Corben of Maidstone, the contractors for Allington, were working at Saltwood. They

excavated the foundations of the earliest hall – unusually Saltwood boasts three great halls, which can be explained as meeting different needs during the varied ownership of the castle. The broken tracery of the windows in the thirteenth-century hall was repaired and those on the south side overlooking the moat were opened up.

To cross the threshold of Saltwood is to enter a rarefied cocoon. The vast moated valley surrounding the castle gives the feeling that once inside the gate one has stepped into a secluded protected world, far removed from the ordinariness of everyday life. It is a haven of tranquil repose that Lord Conway and later both Kenneth Clark and his son Alan found conducive to writing.

Of the Conway building phase, it is the work on what was the Archbishop's

BELOW One of the fourteenth-century D-shaped towers along the line of the outer bailey wall.

hall and audience chamber that is the most spectacular. A huge room with a handsome carved ceiling executed by Hythe Cabinet Works, it is raised above a massive vaulted undercroft. In 1936 Conway wrote to Tilden, 'If you want to mend what should be one of the finest great halls in England, come down to Saltwood at once.'[178] Tilden even carved some of the corbels himself. A mason immortalized Lady (Iva) Conway on one of the corbels. When Iva was widowed once again, she finished the work as a memorial to her second husband, filling it with fine furnishings, so that it became 'an enormous antiquaries parlour, filled with tapestries, church furniture, choir stalls and altar rails'.[179]

BELOW The audience chamber, restored by Lady Conway in memory of Lord Conway.

The Kenneth Clarks first saw Saltwood Castle advertised for sale in *Country Life*. They had lived at Lympne (a mere 4 miles/6.5 kilometres away) before the Second World War but 'To our astonishment . . . we had never even heard of it . . . I had always wanted to live in a gothic house – perhaps some instinct left over from Winchester.' On that occasion it was withdrawn from sale, but by chance a few years later the Clarks found themselves in Folkestone, where they ran into Lord Queensberry, who informed them, 'Lady Conway is dead. You must go over and buy Saltwood.' On arrival, after pulling a rusty bell, they were greeted by Iva's companion, Miss Baird, 'a tricky character' who tried to dismiss them by saying that the castle was sold. Undeterred, the Clarks persisted, saying, 'We should like to buy it.' 'But you haven't looked over it,' she quite reasonably replied; 'besides it is very expensive.' Miss Baird continued to be obstructive, claiming that there was another 'more suitable purchaser'.[180]

Eventually the Clarks bought the castle in 1955. 'Rummaging in the rooms of the Castle after we had bought it was like something in a fairy tale.'[181] As well as being devoted to castles Lady Conway was a keen interior decorator and hoarder of all manner of antiques from pewter to textiles. Lord Clark was later to regret selling many of the things they found.

'Absurd', 'pretentious', 'gothic revival', 'all stairs' were some of the scathing pronouncements by the Clarks' friends on learning of their acquisition. 'The sight of two stone towers made them [their friends] uneasy.'[182]

Apart from turning the audience chamber into a library containing more than ten thousand books, the Clarks did little else to 'Salters', as Lord Clark nicknamed it. The Clarks loved to fill the castle with their friends at weekends. 'Igor Stravinsky, Cecil Beaton, Margot Fonteyn, Paul Robeson made a typically interesting weekend mix.'[183] In due course, Lord Clark handed Saltwood over to his son Alan, whose diaries are littered with exclamations of his deep attachment to the castle. 'What an incredible, marvellous, romantic place Saltwood is, and how I am wedded to it . . . my roots are here in this glorious piece of English medieval history.' [184] Alan Clark died in 1999 and is buried in the garden within the castle walls. His widow, Jane, still lives in the castle.

ABOVE The thirteenth-century cellar beneath the audience chamber.

OPPOSITE The dining room in the gatehouse.

NOTES

SALTWOOD CASTLE

170 Philip Tilden, *True Remembrances: The Memoirs of an Architect*,
    Country Life, 1954, p. 164

171 Stephen Robinson, *The Remarkable Lives of Bill Deedes*, Little
    Brown & Co., 2008

172 Kenneth Clark, *The Other Half: A Self-Portrait*, John Murray,
    1977, p. 187

173 *The Times*, 19 December 1930

174 Kenneth Clark, *The Other Half: A Self-Portrait*, John Murray,
    1977

175 Sir Martin Conway to his sister, Conway Papers, Cambridge
    University Library

176 Kenneth Clark, *The Other Half: A Self-Portrait,* John Murray,
    1977, p. 187

177 Ibid.

178 Philip Tilden, *True Remembrances: The Memoirs of an Architect*,
    Country Life, 1954, p. 164

179 Ibid., pp. 187–8

180 Ibid., pp. 184–5

181 Ibid., p. 188

182 Ibid, pp. 188–9

183 Colin Clark, *Younger Brother, Younger Son*, Harper Collins,
    1997, p. 23

184 Alan Clark, *Diaries: Into Politics*, Weidenfeld & Nicolson, 2000,
    p. 96

LEEDS CASTLE
KENT

'The very fact that water passes under arches turns Leeds Castle into a Kentish Venice. By moonlight the solid walls have no substance; they drift. They seem scarcely moored,' wrote Vita Sackville-West.[185] The stirring battlemented silhouette of the castle rising from two islands in a lake in a fold of the foothills of the North Downs is like the embodiment of an Arthurian legend. 'It might have been created by Tennyson or Walter Scott', wrote H.V. Morton.[186]

The earliest remains still extant of Leeds Castle, near Maidstone, Kent, date from the late thirteenth century, when it was bought by Edward I's wife, Queen Eleanor of Castile. An earlier castle had been built in the early twelfth century by Robert de Crevecoeur. It remained a royal residence for the next three hundred years until the reign of Edward VI. It subsequently became the home of the Culpepers, the Fairfaxes and the Wykeham Martins. Froissart waited upon Richard II 'in his beautiful place called Leeds Castle', and Edward II besieged the castle because its castellan had declined to admit Queen Isabella, 'the she-wolf of France'.[187]

LEFT Lady Baillie with her daughters, Pauline and Susan, painted in the Thorpe Hall at Leeds Castle by Etienne Drian in 1948.

RIGHT Leeds Castle.

But Leeds Castle had fallen into a parlous state by 1925, when Fairfax Wykeham Martin advertised it for rent at an annual sum of £1,000, plus 5 per cent outlay for improvements. The castle had not been lived in for some years, and it was more than a century since any major work had been undertaken. Not surprisingly a tenant did not materialize. Wykeham Martin decided to sell, on one condition: the buyer had to have Kentish connections.

'The news that the loveliest and most fairy castle in England, perhaps in the world, has been sold inevitably interests thousands of people.' Thus was the sale reported in *Country Life* in 1927 by Sir Martin Conway, who had himself recently restored Allington Castle (see page 74), just a few miles distant.

The purchasers were the Hon. Mrs Wilson Filmer,[188] a 26-year-old Anglo-American heiress, and her second husband, Arthur Wilson Filmer. Born in 1899 as Olive Paget, Mrs Wilson Filmer was the daughter of Almeric Paget, later to become the 1st and last Baron Queensborough, and his first wife, Pauline, the daughter and heiress of Hon. William C. Whitney.

The Wilson Filmers were looking for somewhere suitable to use as a weekend country house within striking distance of London. Fortunately, as far as the Wykeham Martin condition was concerned, Mr Wilson Filmer was descended through his maternal grandmother from the old Kentish family of Filmer of East Sutton Park, near Maidstone. His most illustrious antecedent was Sir Robert Filmer (1588–1653), author of *The Patriarcha or the Natural Power of Kings* and exponent of the divine right of kings.

The Wilson Filmers bought Leeds Castle in 1927 with 3,200 acres/1,294 hectares for £180,000, expecting to spend £100,000 on it. They immediately embarked on an ambitious transformation of the castle and its environs into a smart up-to-the-minute backdrop for weekend house parties. As a wealthy American, Olive was used to comfort and she swiftly installed six new bathrooms, each clad from top to bottom in a different coloured marble. Another innovation characteristic of the period was the reincarnation of the chapel as a music room. 'A cupboard housed a huge radiogram; another was fitted out to hold all the records. The radiogram was controlled from the Large Drawing Room and the Saloon where loud speakers were installed.'[189] A chic ebony sprung floor was laid on beams for dancing in the saloon.

The architect Owen Little was responsible for the elegant discreet lodges, the renovation of the stable yard and the internal reorganization under the direction of the French decorator Armand Albert Rateau (1882–1938). Rateau employed more than two hundred craftsmen in his French workshop and worked for other wealthy Americans in France and America, but is best known for decorating the Parisian apartment and two country houses of the French fashion designer Pierre Lanvin. Little drew up the plans for Leeds in London before sending them to Paris for Rateau's approval.

The castle was a hive of activity, employing dozens of local builders as well as several French and Italian craftsmen imported by Rateau. The foreign workers travelled weekly from London by train in a special Southern Railway coach emblazoned 'Leeds Castle only' and then by local bus service, staying in local lodgings. The workmen toiled long hours, relying on candles and oil lamps after dusk had fallen.

Logistically the restoration of a castle situated in the middle of a lake was a challenging project: vast quantities of building materials and rubbish had to be carted to and fro across the water. The solution was to erect a temporary bridge spanning the lake and carrying a light railway. A works office was constructed on floating pontoons.

Rateau was clearly extremely sympathetic to the antiquity of the castle and Little is known to have had a great interest in traditional building methods. Together they subtly reinvented the castle with carefully considered embellishments and additions, such as antique tiles and carved beams executed by Italian and French carvers on site. One particularly

LEFT The temporary bridge and railway track over the moat.

BELOW Workmen's huts alongside the Gloriette during the restoration.

interesting introduction was the strapwork plaster ceiling taken from moulds of a ceiling in the Victoria and Albert Museum that had been removed from the house of Sir Paul Pinder (c.1565–1650) in Bishopsgate Without before its demolition in 1890. Another was the installation of panelling removed from the library of the seventeenth-century Thorpe Hall, near Peterborough, and used at Leeds in the principal drawing room, where 'hundreds of small pieces were fitted together like a jigsaw'.[190] 'As a connoisseur and collector, Filmer was well known to the [architectural salvage] trade.'[191] It is tempting to think that Olive sought the advice of her uncle, the 6th Marquess of Anglesey, who restored

and completely redecorated Beaudesert in Staffordshire after a fire in 1909. 'As with Beaudesert, this [Leeds] castle restoration is urbane and suave,'[192] opines the architectural historian John Harris.

Rateau was also responsible for totally transforming the Fountain Court. He designed and installed a sixteenth-century-style half-timbered screen to house a new oak staircase made in his French workshops and reassembled by French carpenters on site, against the south wall of the Fountain Court. The down pipes were adorned with Tudor roses, scallop shells and wildfowl. The newel post topped with the figure of a crusader was carved from a single tree

OPPOSITE The Great Stairs.

LEFT AND BELOW The central courtyard of the Gloriette was refurbished by Armand Albert Rateau, who installed a sixteenth-century-style half-timbered screen in order to house a new spiral staircase and provide easy access between two floors in this part of the castle.

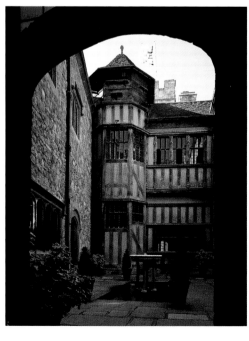

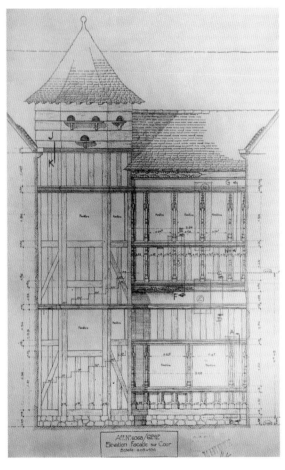

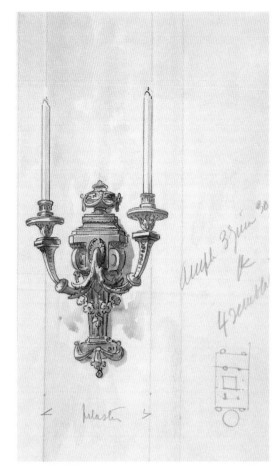

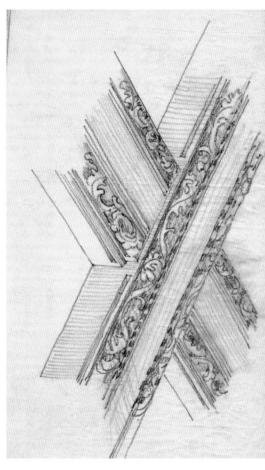

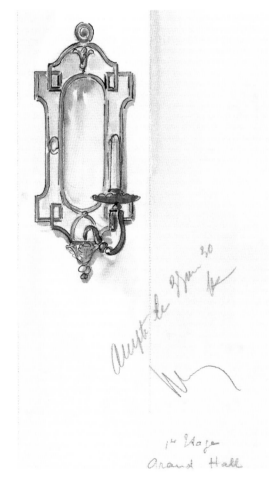

LEFT Various designs by
Armand Albert Rateau for
light fittings, beams and the
courtyard of the Gloriette.

RIGHT ABOVE
The morning room.

RIGHT BELOW Italian and
French carvers working on
the beams.

trunk. The staircase is skilfully concealed behind a lath and plaster screen.

The external improvements were just as lavish. They included two *En-Tout-Cas* tennis courts overlooked by a large rustic pavilion. This was thatched with heather brought from Flimwell Park in Sussex and its oak balustrade incorporates timbers taken from an old staircase in the castle. A nine-hole golf course, ten garages, each large enough for three cars, stabling for thirty horses, twelve new glasshouses and a timber-framed fruit store designed to maintain an even temperature were among other improvements. The light railway on the bridge across the moat was employed to move the soil around to create the Wood Garden, which took two years to complete.

In 1937 a heated open-air swimming pool with underwater lights and a wave machine was installed. 'It was the first of its kind . . . moat water was used, being pumped through a filter and circulated continuously.'[193] The adjoining cocktail bar was painted with a mural entitled *Boys Will Be Boys*, showing the Prime Minister, Neville Chamberlain, skating on a pond covered in thin ice and surrounded by statues of buxom ladies being carried away. They were labelled respectively 'The Rape of Austria', 'The Rape of Czechoslovakia' and 'The Rape of Abyssinia'. Hiding in the background were two naughty urchins, recognizable as Hitler and Goering, and Duff Cooper and Winston Churchill.[194]

In the manner of an eighteenth-century eccentric, Olive, possibly under the influence of Arthur Wilson Filmer, who was a celebrated big game hunter, introduced an exotic assortment of winged, feathered and furry creatures to the park, including at least two zebras, a couple of llamas, and hundreds of ornamental birds including storks and twenty-four flamingos which were placed on the moat – although 'after a few months they flew away'.[195] An extensive range of aviaries was built to house a thrillingly varied assortment of parrots and other tropical birds. She was also very fond of dogs and was responsible for introducing Rhodesian Ridgebacks from Africa to England.

The Wilson Filmers' marriage was over within a couple of years and in 1931 Olive married her third and last husband, Sir Adrian Baillie. It is as Lady Baillie that she is remembered to this day.

It is not known who introduced Lady Baillie to the French decorator Stephane Boudin (1888–1967) in the mid-1930s, but from then until his death they collaborated on the castle interiors, making them much more elaborate and comfortable than they had been in the initial Rateau phase. Boudin, 'the greatest decorator in the world' in the eyes of the diarist Chips Channon,[196] was president of Maison Jansen, the Paris-based interior decorating firm that Jacqueline Kennedy employed to renovate the White House.

Renowned for his keen eye for detail and historical accuracy, Boudin learned his trade initially working for his father, a manufacturer of passmenterie. His two most famous rooms at Leeds Castle are the pale robin-egg-blue painted dining room and Lady Baillie's bedroom, where he distressed the new Louis XIV panelling, scouring it with steel brushes before it was painted a highly sophisticated shade of blue. The castle staff came to dread what became known as 'Boudin weekends' when they were at the beck and call

FAR LEFT The swimming pool being constructed.

LEFT Overlooked by the Maidens' Tower. the pool was filled with filtered water pumped up from the moat.

RIGHT ABOVE Lady Baillie's blue bedroom. created by Stephane Boudin. The panelling was wire-brushed to raise the grain. and then limed and glazed before the blue colour was rubbed in dry and finally beeswaxed.

RIGHT BELOW Lady Baillie's dressing room. designed by Armand Albert Rateau in 1927–9.

BELOW Bridge erected by
Armand-Albert Rateau for the
golfers to cross Broomfield Road.

of Boudin and Lady Baillie, moving furniture around at all hours of the day and night.

'The perfect place to spend a weekend . . . you can fish for giant pike, you can play golf, you can ride and you can listen to Rex Evans singing songs written by Cole Porter,' the *Daily Mail* described the castle shortly after its transformation began.[197] The guest books brim with stars of film and the stage, politicians, royalty and other glamorous figures whom Lady Baillie entertained, including Douglas Fairbanks Senior and Junior, Charlie Chaplin, Errol Flynn, the Woolworths heiress Barbara Hutton, Noël Coward, Edward, Prince of Wales, who came with Mrs Simpson, Queen Marie of Romania, Alfonso XVII of Spain and numerous politicians.

On her death in 1974, Lady Baillie left Leeds Castle to a charitable trust, and Leeds Castle and its grounds are now a leading tourist attraction.

ABOVE LEFT Lady Baillie in 1931.
ABOVE RIGHT Lady Baillie and and the Duke of Kent at her daughter. Pauline's first wedding in 1940.

NOTES

LEEDS CASTLE

185 Vita Sackville-West, *The English Country House*, William Collins, 1945, p. 13

186 H.V. Morton, *I Saw Two Englands: A Record of a Journey Before the War and After the Outbreak of the War in the Year 1939*, Methuen & Co., 1942, p. 57

187 *Country Life*, 28 January 1936

188 The Hon. Olive Paget, born in New York 24 September 1899, the daughter of Almeric Paget, later the 1st Lord Queensborough and his wife, Pauline, née Whitney, m.1st The Hon Charles Winn, m.2nd Arthur Wilson Filmer 1925, m.3rd Sir Adrian Baillie Bt.

189 Joe Cooper (manager of the Estate Yard at Leeds Castle for many years), 'Alterations to the Castle 1926–1974', memoir

190 Alan Bignell, *Lady Baillie at Leeds Castle*, Leeds Castle Enterprises, p. 21

191 John Harris, *Moving Rooms: The Trade in Architectural Salvage*, Yale University Press, 2007, p. 75

192 Ibid.

193 Joe Cooper (manager of the Estate Yard at Leeds Castle for many years), 'Alterations to the Castle 1926–1974', memoir

194 Alan Bignell, *Lady Baillie at Leeds Castle*, Leeds Castle Enterprises, p. 56

195 Joe Cooper (manager of the Estate Yard at Leeds Castle for many years), 'Alterations to the Castle 1926–1974', memoir

196 Alan Bignell, *Lady Baillie at Leeds Castle*, Leeds Castle Enterprises, p. 54

197 *The Daily Mail*, 18 September 1928

CASTELL GYRN
DENBIGHSHIRE

LEFT Castell Gyrn, which John Taylor
built for himself between 1977 and
1982, is set high in the Clwydian range
of hills near Ruthin, Denbighshire,
North Wales.

ABOVE Stained-glass window of
Alice Liddell (Alice in Wonderland) by
Patrick Reyntiens.

Anyone glimpsing the blunt tower of Castell Gyrn rising out of the trees on the Clwydian hills 900 feet/274 metres above Ruthin in North Wales could be forgiven for assuming it is the legacy of a romantically inclined eighteenth-century landowner adorning his land with a fashionable eye-catcher. The reality is that it was built 'not in say 1777 but in 1977', writes Edward Hubbard,[198] as a weekend house by the late John Taylor.

Taylor was then senior partner of Chapman Taylor Partners, one of the biggest post-war commercial architectural practices. Over the years the practice has been responsible for many large modern buildings, its first notable one being New Scotland Yard, erected in the early 1960s. Just as the great eighteenth-century baroque architect Sir John Vanbrugh, having grappled with enormous commissions such as Blenheim Palace in Oxfordshire, designed a small castle for himself in Greenwich, so Taylor built Castell Gyrn for his own use. And what is paramount about Castell Gryn and its grounds is the fun Mr Taylor so clearly had creating his dream rural idyll.

'Like so many architects trained in such modernist schools as the Architectural Association in the late 1940s and early 1950s, John Taylor seems to have turned back to his true roots with a sense of relief after his years in the wilderness of modernism . . . few architects in the late 1970s might have been expected to make the imaginative leap which involved the building of a mock castle to stand beside such monuments as Penrhyn and Gwyrch,' writes *Country Life*.[199]

Castell Gyrn is built of the local grey granite and has a rugged robust appearance evoking ancient Welsh castles. It is situated in sublimely beautiful wild landscape with far-reaching views across the Vale of Clwyd to Snowdonia, the sea at Aberele and the hills of mid-Wales. A charming feature is the rough surface of the granite walls on the internal staircase, a subtle reminder that this is a castle.

The building was initially cruciform in plan with a kitchen and hall, three small bedrooms with bathrooms and a garage underneath. Later a new wing was erected with a terrace and a lookout tower, and an annexe at the rear with a housekeeper's flat and more garages were completed in 1984.

The Taylor family's association with the site dates back to the 1930s, when John's parents bought the field the castle now stands in and put a caravan there, which they used for picnics with John and his sister, Geraldine. It was not until 1955 that they were granted outline planning permission for a bungalow. This was still valid in 1976, but John Taylor's design for a castle

was initially rejected. Following an appeal supported by Lord Esher, a past president of RIBA, and the great Welsh folly builder Clough Williams-Ellis, permission was granted. Then the local authority objected that the proposed castellation contravened building regulations, as the battlements were not high enough to act as parapets. Ingeniously John Taylor applied to the Queen for a 'Licence to Crenellate', seeking permission to 'embattel, kernel and machicolate' the walls. The Privy Council concluded that this was not a matter for Her Majesty to decide alone, and after five months' further deliberation, it decided that it could not advise her to exercise the Royal Prerogative, since the issue of such licences became extinct in the reign of Edward IV. Eventually, after another appeal, the planners relented.

The whole place is imbued with the spirit of someone who loved thinking up just one more little architectural embellishment and commissioning an artist-craftsman to execute it. Even the castle's notepaper was designed by that great engraver and typographer Reynolds Stone, shortly before his death. A particularly delightful quirky detail is the three keystones to the arches of the first prospect tower, with carved faces by Nicholas Wood of Idris Williams, Elfred Hughes and John Griffith, the foreman and two partners of the Denbigh building firm of Hughes Griffith Co., which built the castle. Also adorning the exterior are a carved coat of arms by Simon Winter, three carved slate plaques by Jonah Jones of Penrhyndeudraeth and, positioned high up on the side of the tower, a circular niche containing a classical bust.

The grounds, dotted with witty and imaginative eye-catchers, are very much in the spirit of an eighteenth-century pleasure garden. It cannot be a coincidence that Taylor was educated at Stowe School in Buckinghamshire, which is famous for the landscape garden created by Lord Cobham in the eighteenth century. It cannot be a coincidence that Taylor was educated at Stowe School in Buckinghamshire, famous for its landscape garden created by Lord Cobham in the eighteenth century. Taylor was at one time chairman of the school governors and

no doubt found the follies and monuments that adorn the garden a great source of inspiration.

Following John Taylor's death in 2005 the castle was sold. At first the new owners used it as a holiday home but subsequently they decided to make it their main residence and engaged Donald Insall Associates to make internal alterations as well as enlarging the castle. 'We tried several different options, including adding a second storey on to the existing single-storey wing,' recalls Caroline Blakeley of Donald Insall.[200] This would have detracted from the imposing mass of the

OPPOSITE A recumbent stone ram by Simon Winter acts as a sentinel overlooking the Vale of Clwyd.

BELOW A battlemented tower.

LEFT The entrance approach. To the left is the original tower of 1977: to the right, the later additions of viewing terraces, garages and a staff flat.

BELOW A small vegetable and
rose garden abuts the rear of
the castle.

OPPOSITE The face of Idris
Williams, the mason who
built Castell Gryn, carved in a
keystone by Nicholas Wood.

tower, which has become a local landmark. Eventually it was decided to repeat the single-storey wing and prospect tower, rotating them 90 degrees around the central axis of the plan of the castle and creating a new wing along the north-eastern side at right angles to its original.

From the moment one drives through the twisted wrought-iron gates by Anthony Robinson there is something to beguile wherever one looks, whether it be the proud stone ram carved by Simon Winter that sits like a sentinel below the tower; the little stone building decorated inside with shells by Charlotte Kerr-Wilson; the circular stone enclosure containing a 'crossbow' sundial by Peter Parkinson; or a triumphal arch surmounted by the royal arms which once were on Clerkenwell Police Station. Near the entrance from the road there is a minuscule gatehouse dedicated to Alice of Wonderland; inside there is a small stained-glass roundel by Patrick Reyntiens of her real-life inspiration, Alice Liddell. There is even an obelisk entitled the Burrows Monument, named after the local building inspector whose obtuse attitude towards the crenellations gave rise to the petition to the Queen.

The sublime setting of Castell Gryn in the North Wales countryside coupled with its fairy-tale tower combine to make it an important late twentieth-century example of the great English picturesque tradition.

NOTES

CASTELL GYRN
198 Edward Hubbard, *Clwyd* (Pevsner Architectural Guides: Buildings of Wales), Yale University Press, 1986
199 *Country Life*, 28 January 1988
200 Ibid.

BRAYLSHAM CASTLE
EAST SUSSEX

Braylsham Castle is an architectural enigma. At first sight, it appears to be a compact, moated medieval castle nestling on an island in a lake in a hidden valley deep in the richly wooded landscape of the Sussex Weald. It could have come straight from the sketchbook of a Regency clergyman: one can almost imagine the notes of the enthusiastic antiquary in the margins. But there never was such a painting, because, ancient and pretty though it seems, Braylsham is a newborn castle, completed only in 1998.

Glimpsed from the hill above it has every appearance of having evolved over time, with different historic layers. The castle also seems larger than it really is, partly because it occupies most of the island it stands on. Only as one gets close does the diminutive scale become apparent.

The man who conceived this remarkable fantasy-like castle is the multi-talented John Mew. He learned to fly a Tiger Moth at eighteen, and has long been a keen sailor, competing in the first post-war challenge for the Americas Cup in 1958. He designed, built and raced his own sports car and was one of the last private Formula One entrants, twice breaking the lap record at Brands Hatch. He also pioneered a branch of orthodontics known as orthotropics.

For such a pioneering character a 'phoney castle', as he teasingly describes Braylsham, seems a curious choice of dwelling.[201] But Mr Mew has deeply held philosophical views on what exactly constitutes the ideal way to live. His researches into social anthropology led him to the conclusion that a castle on an island is the ideal dwelling: a castle with its traditional accoutrements, such as look-out turrets, and a drawbridge 'give an innate feeling of security. A modern house is just a sort of block.' His wife, Jo, a physiotherapist, spends her days working in hospitals and did not want to come home to another 'sterile environment'.

One of the most remarkable aspects of Braylsham is that a great deal of the construction work, from the creation of the lake to the actual building of the castle, was executed by the Mews themselves. Mr Mew had already honed his building skills on his last house, a derelict mill adjacent to Braylsham, which he bought in 1987 and subsequently restored with the help of Stephen Langer of Stephen Langer Associates, who later helped him to design Braylsham.

The Mews realized that to obtain planning permission would be something of a challenge in an area of outstanding natural beauty, so they engaged

LEFT Braylsham Castle sits deep in a
hidden valley in the Sussex Weald.

BELOW The decorative Gothic
Revival windows of the great hall
were reused from a redundant
church in Carmarthenshire.

a planning consultant, Peter Kember of Kember Loudon Williams. Initially they sought outline permission to replace a derelict two-up, two-down cottage on a site higher up the valley with a four-bedroom, two-garaged house, but later reapplied to re-site the dwelling on a spit of land that is now the island. 'I had always wanted to live by water.' Obtaining this permission took six months.

Next, the detailed plans for the castle were submitted, only to be refused. 'The planning officers thought I was going to build a Disney-style structure,' says Mr Mew, 'so I bribed the planning committee by inviting them round for tea and crumpets to show them the plans without the officers interfering – they loved it.' Mr Mew commissioned a watercolour artist, George Hawkins, to paint an impression of what the castle would look like and sent a copy to each member of the planning committee. The huge file of supportive letters grew. The decision took fifteen months.

On his sixtieth birthday his wife gave him a digger and he set about clearing the landscape. He felled trees, made the lake by damming the two streams that run through the valley and built the island. The landscaping took two and a half years and involved moving more than 12,000 tonnes of soil. There were two major setbacks when rain dislodged the excavated earth.

Work began in 1993 and was eventually finished in 1998. The Mews employed a full-time bricklayer for three years and a stonemason for two. A team of carpenters made the skeleton. 'We cleared and levelled the site ourselves and installed all the reinforced concrete girders. I realized that our land included the ideal setting for something special. There are very few such sites in southern England and I thought that it really did deserve something beautiful – the fall of the ground, the shape, the line, everything was right.'

The castle is split into three distinct sections: the tower, the great hall and a half-timbered structure. Mr Mew wanted to create the illusion of antiquity and so built the half-timbered end at an angle, jutting out over the moat. Inside, the floors are deliberately set at a slight slant. 'I hate right angles. The brickie was very precise about all the details; it was with great difficulty that I managed to persuade him to be less rigid.' The highly romantic moated fourteenth-century Ightham Mote, a property of the National Trust near Sevenoaks in Kent, was an important source of inspiration.

'I worked on the basis that because it is in a lake one side would be likely to have subsided over the centuries and I wanted it to look as if the foundations had sunk down.' Mr Mew achieved this by getting his carpenters to lower one end of the roof, standing on top of the adjacent hill and shouting instructions at them until they got it right.

'Usually within the design of an old house there are accretions of history built up over time, but Braylsham is a sort of potted history,' says Mr Langer. 'Mr Mew wanted an instant air of antiquity, whereas I was more inclined to let the weather age it over time.'

The Mews used sandstone – which they gathered up themselves from their land – for the initial construction, including the base of the great hall. Then, when they had exhausted their reserves of the sandstone, they opted for Dorset Green stone for the remaining two-thirds of the castle. It proved cheaper to bring this up from the West Country than to buy locally sourced stone.

The approach to the castle, also meticulously planned by Mr Mew, sustains the sense of drama as the drive proceeds into the valley. After the initial thrilling glimpse from above the valley, the drive descends via a circuitous route that affords little glimpses of the castle rising up out of the lake. As one nears the castle, the drive goes over a little bridge straddling one of the streams. The Mews eschewed any idea of a garden, as they felt it would vie for attention with the castle.

All the family was involved in the planning of the internal layout. 'We played around with bits of paper with our three children.' The interior is laid out over four floors and includes a cellar and an integral two-car garage. The different levels are connected by two spiral staircases within the towers.

RIGHT John Mew carving
decorative corbels for his
great hall.

None of the rooms is very big; the double-height great hall measures only 16 x 26 feet/5 x 8 metres. There are five 'odd triangular bedrooms' leading off each other with en-suite bathrooms; a master bedroom and a dressing room; and a drawing room, a kitchen and Mr Mew's small office, which opens off the kitchen – 'I wanted to be in the heart of the house.' A striking detail of the first-floor drawing room is the floor-to-ceiling window overlooking the lake.

An important element of the overall conceit is the inclusion of several architectural details salvaged from disused churches, such as the Gothic Revival windows in the great hall. A major setback was the theft from the building site of some stained glass and windows from two church halls in Bristol. This held the Mews up by eighteen months as they sought replacements. They wrote to every diocese in England and contacted all the leading architectural salvage dealers, and eventually found substitutes from a redundant church in Carmarthenshire. 'The windows we got are more elaborate than we had originally envisaged but by that stage we were desperate.' The floor and steps into the great hall from the kitchen came from a demolished church in Tunbridge Wells.

The overall cost of the castle was kept well under £400,000, which can partly be explained by the very hands-on approach of the Mews. For instance, they jointly cast the treads for the spiral staircase in the main tower. 'To commission them in cut stone would have been prohibitively expensive. A firm that does artificial stone was going to charge £1,200 to make the mould and a further £100 per tread,' says Mr Mew. 'I went to the factory and decided we could make them ourselves.' Undaunted, they set to work making a mould. Their bricklayer helped to mix the correct colour using reconstituted stone. To make each step took about two days (there are seventy-eight steps). In true Mew style each step was carefully made to look worn, as if feet had been pounding up and down the tower for centuries.

In realizing their very personal vision in this individual way the Mews have crafted a building that takes a unique place in the ever-evolving tradition of castle building.

NOTES

BRAYLSHAM CASTLE
201 All quotations in this chapter are from Amicia de Moubray,
article in *Country Life*, 22 February 2007

BALLONE
INVERNESS·SHIRE

Of the many Scottish tower houses and castles brought back to life in recent years, Ballone Castle, near Tain in Inverness-shire, is one of the most spectacular examples, a model restoration by an architect at the peak of his career. Dramatically situated on the edge of a steep cliff overlooking the Moray Firth near Portmahomack, Tarbat Ness, it soars out of the flat landscape, proudly surveying all in its ken. Its roofless shell first made a striking impression on the architect Lachlan Stewart at the age of seventeen. Several years later, he and his wife, Annie, who had met at the Edinburgh School of Art, armed themselves with MacGibbon and Ross's five-volume *The Castellated and Domestic Architecture of Scotland*[202] and set out to find a castle to renovate as their home. 'One wild night we found ourselves near Ballone and we decided to see if anything was still standing,' Stewart recalls.[203]

Immediately captivated, they persuaded Ballone's farmer owner to sell within a day. Ballone's advanced state of decrepitude – by the time the Stewarts purchased it, one part of the structure was propped up on a single stone or, as an engineer described it, 'balanced on a sugar lump' – would have deterred all but the hardiest and most dedicated conservationists. The Stewarts fitted this description. Their first marital home, Plockton lighthouse on the west coast of Scotland, had no electricity and was only accessible by boat.

Stewart has castle restoration in his genes: his great-grandfather was John MacRae-Gilstrap of Eilean Donan fame and his grandfather was a stonemason. He studied under the late architectural historian and pioneering conservationist Colin McWilliam, before working for Ian Hurd and Partners, an architectural practice widely acclaimed for its knowledge of the Scottish vernacular. Under the umbrella of Anta, a company set up by the Stewarts in the 1980s, Stewart runs a successful architectural practice renowned for sympathetic historic restorations throughout Scotland as well as designing new shooting lodges, hotels and visitor centres. His first solo commission was the visitor centre at Eilean Donan.

Having often visited Eilean Donan as a child it seemed 'a natural thing to do to restore a castle', says Lachlan Stewart. He recently discovered a family tree at Eilean Donan with an image of Ballone, which showed that in the eighteenth century a Mackenzie of Ballone had married a MacRae of Eilean Donan.

LEFT Ballone, a sixteenth-century castle restored from a ruin by Lachlan and Annie Stewart.

ABOVE Last inhabited at the end of the seventeenth century, Ballone was a roofless shell before its restoration.

LEFT There is a charming simplicity to the interiors. Clockwise from top left: bedroom; the main room in the extension added in 2008; the great hall.

RIGHT The enclosed garden perches on the cliff top.

Ballone is a fine example of a typical Z-plan castle with one round and one square tower. Believed to have been built by a line of the Earls of Ross, it is first recorded in the early seventeenth century as belonging to the Dunbars of Tarvit. In 1623 it was bought by the Mackenzies, who became Earls of Cromartie in 1703. They abandoned it in favour of Tarbart House in the late seventeenth century.

Initially the Stewarts had to grapple for three years with Historic Scotland, convincing them that enough of the castle remained for it to be viable to change its listed status from that of a monument to a residence. Over the following years in the mid-1990s the structure was restored – 'its essential elements have not changed at all' – while the Stewarts, with an expanding family of young children, lived on site, first in a caravan and then in an adjacent hut.

The entry to Ballone is through a small arched entrance door from which ascends a steep spiral staircase, emerging in a lofty great hall which was the hub of family life until 2008.

In 2008 the Stewarts added an extension over the seventeenth-century vaults. This is roofed in handsome

OPPOSITE
Looking out to
the Moray Firth.

FAR LEFT
A corbelled-out
bartizan crowns
the corners and
has a shot hole
and stone roof.

LEFT The rugged
exterior of Ballone
is painted in a
sandy yellowy
limewash, which
makes the castle
stand out from
afar in the
landscape.

huge Caithness slates, and for the walls Stewart used Zeigle (terracotta) blocks as an inexpensive alternative to stone – they have a honeycomb structure and are both load bearing and insulating. The walls are finished in rough-cast plaster, creating an organic moulded texture. The main space is one commodious room in the new wing which the Stewarts now use for everyday living. 'We live in the space much as it would have been lived in three hundred years ago.' It is a democratic way of living that traditionally was at the very heart of Scottish clan life, with every rank eating at the same table, but disappeared in Georgian and Victorian society.

The great hall and the exterior of Ballone are painted in a sandy yellowy limewash, and elsewhere the internal walls are painted in warm neutral tones of limewash. In choosing these finishes the Stewarts drew upon their extensive travels in Italy, where they observed that painted stone is widely used to unify architecture.

Lachlan Stewart's objectives are to 'promote a unified aesthetic, so that furnishing and even the garden all speak to each other'. This dictum is much in evidence at Ballone where, despite the rugged appearance both externally and internally, the interiors exude a pleasing warmth. The furnishings are a medley of sturdy Arts and Crafts-inspired furniture designed by the Stewarts, lightened by the judicious use of Anta fabrics and carpets, which inject dashes of colour and pattern. Some of the larger items of furniture had to be literally dropped into place before the roofs were put on.

The castle's magical situation overlooking a huge expanse of sea accounts for the intense quality of the light that streams in through the diminutively scaled windows. 'The sea adds a luminescence. It is as if we are constantly surrounded by snow on the ground,' Annie Stewart says. Indeed Lachlan Stewart likens a Scottish castle such as Ballone to an igloo carved out of blocks of snow. There is an honest robustness to such a structure, which is entirely appropriate in the wilds of Scotland.

Lachlan Stewart has used Ballone as a laboratory, endlessly experimenting with different ideas on the fabric. As he says, 'Every generation tackles restoration in a different way whilst creating a modern home in a medieval shell.'

NOTES
BALLONE
202 Mary Miers, Country Life, 26 January 2006
203 All quotations in this chapter are from a conversation with Amicia de Moubray in 2011

CORROUR LODGE
INVERNESS-SHIRE

Corrour, in the Scottish Highlands on the edge of Rannoch Moor, is a bravely modern interpretation of a Scottish lodge, like many castles planned internally around a great hall. The striking impression on arrival at what must be one of the most innovative domestic buildings erected in Scotland in the twenty-first century is heightened by the long journey necessary to reach it. Indeed so remote is Corrour station, the highest in Britain – Corrour is at an altitude of 1,269 feet/387 metres – that the guard has to be warned well in advance for the train to stop. The alternative route by road culminates in a 12-mile/19-kilometre drive from the main road on which there is a tantalizing glimpse across Loch Ossian of its extraordinary granite and glass outline just visible through the trees, set against the hills of Beinn Eibhinn and Cnoc Dearg. This all adds considerably to the experience.

The Lodge at Corrour was built in 2003 for a Swedish academic by the Boston-based Israeli-Canadian architect Moshe Safdie. Safdie studied architecture at McGill University and then went on to spend a year with the American architect Louis Kahn, before returning to Montreal to oversee the master plan for Expo '67. Among Safdie's public commissions in Israel, Canada and America are the Salt Lake City Main Public Library, the Kauffman Center for the Performing Arts in Kansas City and the Crystal Bridges Museum of American Art in Bentonville, Arkansas. Corrour is not only his sole work in Britain: it is his only domestic commission.

An earlier nineteenth-century lodge at Corrour was torn down by Sir John Stirling Maxwell six years after he bought the vast Inverness-shire estate in 1891, aged twenty-four. Three years later, perhaps spurred on by the opening of the West Highland railway line to Fort William, the young man commissioned a far more substantial house at the head of Loch Ossian, a granite crowstep-gabled house by Frank College of the Glasgow architects Wharr and College, which was remodelled a few years later by L. and J. Falconer. In 1942 this was ravaged by fire. The remains were largely demolished in 1950, leaving just two wings. These Safdie skilfully swept up into his design: the former schoolroom, game larder and gun room are now two cottages and an estate office, and the chapel is now bedroom accommodation.

Just as Stirling Maxwell entertained large house parties at Corrour, particularly in the summer months, the new owners' main requirement was to have plenty of bedrooms with reception rooms commodious enough to accommodate all their guests, along with the necessary domestic offices and a drying room – a vital prerequisite for any Scottish sporting lodge.

LEFT The striking main façade of Corrour Lodge, designed by Moshe Safdie and completed in 2003.

BELOW A semi-conical glass window
juts out from the dining room.

OPPOSITE The mezzanine floor
has a vast glazed barrel roof. The
sculpture is by Anish Kapoor.

Externally the house is composed of two segments, one a rectilinear block and the other cylindrical, linked by a glazed stairwell. The segments are pierced by glazed etiolated semi-conical triangles which thrust 'up through the masonry like shards of ice',[204] creating the impression – especially effective when seen from the loch through the trees – that the building is soaring skywards.

The remaining granite fragments of the original lodge determined that granite should be the principal building material. It proved impossible to source local granite that could be cut to the right specifications, resulting in the importation of silvery granite from Portugal.

A nephew of the great nineteenth-century collector of rhododendrons Sir Herbert Maxwell, Sir John planted Britain's highest rhododendron garden at Corrour, and below the lodge he installed an imaginative alpine garden with an oval pool in the middle. This little garden brilliantly anchors the new lodge to its site, providing a vital link between its

The interiors at Corrour have a clean
Scandinavian look and are decorated
with twentieth-century and contemporary
furnishings and works of art.
BELOW The drawing room.
RIGHT Top: Bedroom. Centre: Bunk room
designed by film production designer Jon
Bunker. Bottom: A semi-circular library.

BELOW Looking down Loch Ossian, from a corner of the drawing room.

OPPOSITE ABOVE The central hall.

OPPOSITE BELOW The dining-room table is by Hans Olsen and the chairs by Arne Jacobsen.

startlingly crisp lines for such a setting and the sublimely beautiful wild natural landscape beyond. The garden's gentle curving contours soften the somewhat forbidding verticality of the lodge's two tower-like structures.

The curves of the oval pond are echoed in the circular drawing room on ground level in the drum tower, cut into by the sharp-angled base of the pyramid, and they are echoed also in the two ground-floor libraries, which are semi-circular.

The site at the head of Loch Ossian commands a magnificent far-reaching view, which has to a large degree dictated the fenestration of the new lodge. The drawing room, the dining room, the main bedrooms and the main staircase have been designed around vast windows looking on to the wild landscape.

Furniture and pictures have been deliberately kept to the minimum, accentuating the clean bones of the house. The interior designer Suzy Hoodless helped the owners to assemble a fine collection of furniture by leading Scandinavian twentieth-century designers, including Arne Jacobsen's Oxford chairs in the dining room, Finn Juhl's Chieftain sofa of 1949 in the drawing room and an Egg chair by Arne Jacobsen. These are successfully combined with fine antique tapestries, some contemporary English furniture and an outstanding collection of modern art including pieces by Anish Kapoor.

This is a house of surprises, evident from the moment of arrival. There is no monumental entrance porch or even a stately front door, merely an austere granite cloistered Edwardian service court, which opens on to a small entrance hall simply furnished with an eighteenth-century marble-topped console table and a splendid Irish elk's antlers. This in turn gives on to the great hall, from which the principal rooms open through a granite colonnade. It is at this point that one first becomes aware of the compelling views.

Originally the great hall was a much more dramatic space, rising through the height of the house to a glass barrel vault that rolled down from a crenellated parapet. This proved to be an awkward, unfriendly space and has since been modified by the insertion of a new floor, creating an extra reading area with bookshelves and comfortable sofas.

Though Corrour is clearly not a castle in the conventional idiom, its tower-like protuberances, the stern granite structure, its location in the wildly dramatic landscape and the internal layout with the rooms all grouped around a great hall, although contemporary in appearance, adhere to the image of a Scottish castle. The architect's strikingly original use of these features is an illustration of how the castle's traditional aesthetic continues to flourish in the modern architectural age.

ABOVE The discreet entrance to Corrour is through what was originally the Edwardian service court.

RIGHT ABOVE A pair of elk antlers dominate the stark entrance hall.

RIGHT BELOW The great hall, from which the principal rooms open through a granite colonnade.

NOTES
CORROUR LODGE
204 Mary Miers, *The Western Seaboard*, Rutland Press, 2008, and *Country Life*, 26 January 2006.

INDEX

Page numbers in italic refer to captions and/or illustrations

PICTURE ACKNOWLEDGMENTS

The author and publisher thank the following copyright owners for permission to reproduce their illustrations on the pages listed after their names. Every effort has been made to provide correct attributions. Any inadvertent errors or omissions will be corrected in subsequent editions of this book.

a = above b = below c = centre l = left r = right

Amicia de Moubray: 23, 120–21
Bonhams: 98
Bridgeman Art Library: 64r (The Art Workers' Guild Trustees Limited, London), 114 (The Lady Lever Art Gallery/The Estate of Augustus John)
Country Life Picture Library: 2–3, 4–5, 6, 9, 35, 40, 41, 43, 44, 45, 46, 47, 54–5al, ar, bl and br, 56, 62, 63, 64l, 66l, 66–7a and b, 74, 75, 76, 77, 78–9, 84–5, 85, 88, 89, 90, 91, 96–7, 99, 102a and b, 103, 104, 105, 108–9, 111, 112, 113, 122, 123, 124–5, 126, 127, 128, 129, 136, 137, 138, 139, 140, 141, 144, 146–7, 148, 149, 150, 151, 156, 159a, 164, 165, 166, 167, 168–9, 170, 171, 172–3, 174, 176
Corrour Estate: 27, 184, 186, 187, 188–9, 190a, c and b, 190, 191a and b, 192, 193a and b
East Ayrshire Council: 11, 20
Hever Castle, 48–9, 51, 52ar and b, 53, 57, 58, 59, 60, 61
National Trust Images: 13a (Paul Barker), 14 (Alasdair Ogilvie), 16 (Francis Frith Collection), 24 (Susan Witney), 68–9 (Val Corbett), 70, 71 and 72 (Andreas von Einsiedel), 82 (John Hammond), 83 (Dennis Gilbert), 84l, 86l (Chris Gascoigne), 86r (Robert Morris), 87 (Dennis Gilbert), 92a, ar and bl (James Mortimer), 92 br, 93a (James Mortimer), 93ar (Dennis Gilbert), 93bl and br (James Mortimer), 94 (John Hammond), 95 (Andrew Butler)

RIBA Library Drawings and Archives Collections: 65, 132, 133, 134, 135l and r
Mary Evans Picture Library: 110
Michael Shippobottom: 115, 116–7, 119a and b
John Goodall: 100–101
Lachlan Stewart: 1, 179, 180al and ar, 182, 183l and r
Lucinda Lambton: 10l
Richard Surman: 10r
The Selfridges Archive/The History of Advertising Trust Archive: 130
The Queen Elizabeth Castle of Mey Trust: 16, 181
Dylan Thomas: 25l and r, 26, 28
Nick McCann: 30, 31, 34, 36, 37a, c and b, 38, 73
Camera Press: 145
The Times: 21
Sir Robert Worcester: 801
Royal Commission of Ancient and Historical Monuments of Scotland: 106
The National Galleries of Scotland: 107
Leeds Castle Foundation: 152, 153, 155a and b, 157l and r, 158, 159b, 160l and r, 161a and b, 162, 161l and r
Rory Carnegie: 178, 180b, 181
Clive Richards: 19

AUTHOR ACKNOWLEDGMENTS

I am indebted to Michael Hall, who encouraged me from the first with my idea for the book and very kindly read the original draft. Also I can't thank Mary Miers of *Country Life* enough for her never-ending willingness to share her astonishing knowledge of Scottish architecture with me. Justin Hobson of the *Country Life* Picture Library also deserves a special thank you, as does Kirsty Hudson for so kindly introducing me to John Nicoll. But it is my husband, Richard Oldfield, whom I must thank from the bottom of my heart for all the help, advice and encouragement he has given me. My son, Edward, and my stepchildren, Leonora, Christopher and Henry, have all been very patient and helpful.

Many other people have helped over the past few years since I first began thinking about castles, including the following: Jane Clark, Camilla Costello, Jeremy Musson, Annabel Freyberg, John Goodall, Tim Richardson, Karen Howes, Ruth Guilding, Matthew Wilcox, Robert Sackville-West, Adam Nicolson, the ever-patient and helpful staff of the London Library, Lisa Waters of Bamburgh Castle, James Hervey-Bathurst, Laurie Magnus, Robert and Margaret Worcester, Lachlan Stewart, Barbara Hiddleston of the Castle of Mey, Amara Thornton, Nic Fulcher and Victoria Wallace of Leeds Castle, Dylan Thomas, Hugh Meller, Brian Tetlow, Julia and Michael Wigan, Lisbet Rausing, Norman Bachop, who kindly drove me round Northumberland and Scotland visiting many of the castles included in the book, Stephen Calloway, Allan Maclean, James Bettley, Clive Aslet, Thomas Seymour, Michael Shippobottom, Caroline Blakeley, Lucinda Lambton, Rory Carnegie, Philip Dean and Bob MacPherson of Corrour Estate, Timothy Stevens, Timothy Britain-Caitlin, Henrietta Heald, Gavin Stamp, Duncan Leslie and Ann Watt of Hever Castle, Becky Clarke of Frances Lincoln, and Anne Askwith for editing the text with patience and skill.